The Investor's
Self-Teaching Seminars

TRADING
STOCK INDEX
OPTIONS

The Investor's

Self-Teaching Seminars

TRADING STOCK INDEX OPTIONS

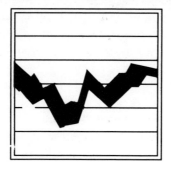

One of a Series of Hands-On Workshops
Dedicated to the Serious Investor

Mikel T. Dodd

Probus Publishing Company
Chicago, Illinois

Dodd, Mikel T.
    Trading stock index options / Mikel T. Dodd.
        p. cm. — (The Investor's self-teaching seminars)
    "One of a series of hands-on workshops dedicated to the serious investor."
    ISBN 0-917253-69-8
    1. Stock index futures.   I. Title.   II. Series.
    HG6043.D64 1988
332.64'52 — dc19   87-32699
                                                                    CIP

ISBN 0-917253-69-8

Printed in the United States of America

BC

    2 3 4 5 6 7 8 9 0

Preface

Serious investors require practical techniques for reducing risk, improving return and liquidity, and translating market predictions into specific investment actions. Stock index options may satisfy all of these needs. Investment professionals have used these powerful instruments since their introduction in 1983 to speculate on market movements or to hedge equity portfolios. Individual investors can easily apply similar strategies after acquiring a working knowledge of index option contracts and strategies.

This book presents an introduction to stock index options. The reader will learn how to integrate index options into a speculative or protective investment program, which index to select, which option to select, how many options to purchase or sell, and much more.

Index options are complex instruments. Careful preparation is required before these options are added to a portfolio. This book is meant to give the reader the information needed to deal with these instruments.

In addition to the fundamentals of index options, applications are also dealt with. Several professional strategies for speculating with index options are discussed in detail, highlighting the return potential and risks, and are dealt with in terms of an individual investor's ability to copy professional techniques. Problems designed to enhance the reader's understanding of speculative strategies are also included with sample solutions provided at the end of the book. Professional portfolio protection (hedging) strategies are also dealt with. The complexities of achieving a good hedge are investigated with an emphasis on practical applications of technical concepts. Once again, sample problems are included.

The mechanics of trading index options are dealt with in terms of:

> Opening an option account
> Executing a transaction
> Maintaining the account
> Sources of information
> Tax considerations

The book concludes with two case studies and two simulations which should further enhance the reader's understanding. Each case study is thoroughly analyzed, emphasizing the complexities of the situation. The simulations illustrate the technical aspects of using stock index options and allow the reader to "participate" by producing necessary calculations or rendering some key decisions.

Serious investors need the best opportunities to manage risk and enhance return. Stock index options are used by professional investors to achieve both goals. This book provides realistic information and practical applications that should allow individual investors to enjoy the benefits of these new investment tools.

CONTENTS

Prologue

BRIAN CHADWICK

Brian Chadwick has been investing in the stock market for several years. Now 35, he feels that his position at work is secure and his portfolio sound. Brian has always invested conservatively—only in blue-chip companies with stable histories—because of his belief that he should avoid high-risk investments until his financial situation was secure. Now that he has achieved that security and has several years of experience investing in equities, he would like to use some of his extra cash to "play the market" a bit.

Brian reads *The Wall Street Journal* daily, and he now feels ready to translate some of his opinions about market movements into investment action. If the return on an investment is high enough, Brian is willing to take on more risk. However, he does not want his initial cash commitment to be a large one.

Brian realizes that his change in attitude towards risk requires some reassessment of his investment objectives, at least for a portion of his portfolio. First, Brian decides that he is satisfied with his current stock holdings. Thus, any funds for speculative investments must be restricted to the $3,000 in his money market fund. However, he feels uncomfortable risking all of the $3,000, so he decides that $2,000 is the maximum amount he is willing to invest.

Given this amount, Brian's alternatives are somewhat limited. Some of Brian's friends suggest investments such as high-growth penny stocks, commodity futures, and stock options. The first two don't appeal to Brian because he has no experience in these markets. His experience has focused on large, New York Stock Exchange-type firms and he wants to apply this experience to his speculative investments, if possible. Investing his $2,000 in penny stocks and commodity futures would feel to Brian just like placing a bet on a roulette wheel.

Stock options seem to have some merit, however. Brian has plenty of experience in equities and follows equity investments daily. He is somewhat familiar with stock options and their risks. The primary problem with this alternative, from Brian's point of view, is that he would have to invest in a single company. How will he select that one company? What information should he base his prediction on— broad market factors that would influence the company's performance or company-specific factors that are hard to discover and act upon? Can he get timely information on that particular firm?

What Brian really wants is an investment that doesn't require him to make company-specific predictions. He wants to bet on broad, widely reported movements in the market, and a stock option investing program would not allow him such latitude. Given the limitations of stock options, Brian decides to invest in a relatively new and promising investment vehicle, stock index options.

STEVE TYSON

Steve Tyson is nearing retirement. For many years he has been accumulating savings and investing them in the stock market. Steve does not consider himself a risk taker, and at this point in his life he is especially cautious. His primary investment goal is protecting what he has earned so far without having to sacrifice the opportunities to profit from a good economy. He has resisted investing in vehicles such as certificates of deposit because of their fixed returns. He believes this strategy protects the value of his portfolio from deterioriation through inflation.

However the recent wild fluctuations in stock prices have caused Steve to reassess his strategy. The wide market shifts obviously concern Steve because he must preserve his nest egg for retirement. He is still adverse to committing a large sum of his retirement fund to CDs, for if inflation returns his position will deteriorate rapidly. He wants to keep investing in corporate equities to hedge against potential inflation. How can he do so and yet avoid or limit the fluctuation of his portfolio's value? A friend recommends stock options as hedging vehicles.

Stock options can be used to augment stock returns during periods in which a company's stock price is expected to decline slightly or remain neutral. Stock options can also be used to safeguard against dramatic declines in stock prices. The problem with dedicating an entire portfolio to this strategy is that many different options would be involved, requiring significant transaction expenses. Furthermore, some of the companies represented in Steve's portfolio do not have listed options available. He decides that these drawbacks outweigh the benefits of stock options. At his broker's suggestion, Steve investigates stock index options as an alternative investment.

The complications encountered by Brian Chadwick and Steve Tyson are typical of difficulties facing serious investors in today's fast-paced market. (We'll return to the cases of Brian and Steve in Chapter 5.) But as their examples illustrate, individual investors can place market ''bets'' or protect a portfolio easily and inexpensively with stock index options. This book is intended as a guide to investors who want to learn how to include index options in their personal portfolios and thereby, share the benefits these instruments are providing professional traders every day.

Chapter One

INTRODUCTION

Rarely has a new financial instrument generated as much excitement and sheer volume of trading as stock index options. In less than four years these powerful new securities have experienced daily volume exceeding hundreds of thousands of contracts in the largest index option market. These investment tools have enjoyed extraordinary development because of the opportunities for market speculation and portfolio management they provide professional and individual investors.

The investment problems highlighted in the prologue are typical of the difficulties serious investors encounter in today's fast-paced market. Now, an individual investor can easily and inexpensively apply professional index option strategies to place market "bets" or protect a portfolio. This book serves as a guide for the investor who wants to learn how to include index options in his or her personal portfolio management and thereby share the benefits these instruments are providing professional traders.

HISTORY

On March 11, 1983, the Chicago Board Options Exchange (CBOE) opened trading for options on the Standard & Poor's (S & P) 100.

Over 4,500 contracts changed hands that day. Today, average daily volume on the S & P 100 frequently exceeds 1 million contracts. OEX (the ticker symbol for S & P 100 index options) volume regularly averages 75 percent of total trading volume and has topped 80 percent of daily volume on the CBOE, which is the largest options exchange in the country.

When the options were introduced, exchange planners gave considerable thought to which indexes should be included. For the new contracts to be successful, the index selected had to be useful for many different types of investors. Also, publishers of some indexes considered them proprietary and would not allow exchanges to trade contracts on these indexes. The Dow Jones Industrial Average, for example, is not currently optionable.

The OEX was selected as the first index option because it met the demand of institutional investors for a market hedging tool. This index option also served the needs of speculators who wanted to translate market opinions into investment action easily and inexpensively. The dramatic growth of the OEX underscores the popularity of this broad-based index.

As the index option market developed, options on subindexes were introduced. These cover certain segments of the market, such as oil and gas, and transportation indexes. Subindex options are useful for investors with portfolios heavily weighted with stocks in these particular market sectors as well as speculators with an opinion on the future of specific sectors.

The first subindex option, the Amex Computer Technology Index, was introduced on August 26, 1983. Many more were introduced shortly thereafter, but were not all accepted by the market. Today, broad-based index options are still, by far, the more popular contracts.

Currently, options on 12 indexes are traded. Seven of these are broad-based and five are subindexes. These are listed in Exhibit 1-1.

Index option activity is reported daily in major newspapers and weekly in *Barrons*. Exhibit 1-2 is the listing from *The Wall Street Journal* for Monday, December 1, 1986.

Exhibit 1-1
Optional Indexes

Index*	Exchange
S&P 100 Index (OEX)	CBOE
S&P 500 Index (SPX)	CBOE
Airline Index (XAI)	AMEX
Computer Technology Index (XCI)	AMEX
Gold/Silver Index (XAU)	PHIL
Major Market Index (XMI)	AMEX
NYSE Beta Index (NHB)	NYSE
NYSE Composite (NYA)	NYSE
National OTC Index (XOC)	PHIL
Oil Index (XOI)	AMEX
Technology Index (PSE)	PACF
Value Line Composite (XVL)	PHIL

*Ticket symbol given in parentheses.

PREVIEW OF APPLICATIONS

Index options give investors a wide range of alternatives for market speculation. Using these options, overall market opinion can be translated into an investment action quickly and easily for a relatively modest amount of money. The mechanics of doing this are the same whether you are predicting a rise or a fall in the market. If you have an opinion about a specific segment of the market, this can also be translated into investment action if that segment is represented by an optionable index.

Index options may also be used to overcome problems in the timing of receipts and disbursements of investment funds. For example, an investor who expects to receive a sum of money in the future may establish a market position using options before the funds are received. The option position will allow this investor to participate in any possible market gains even though the funds are still outstanding.

Exhibit 1-2
Option Listing
Wall Street Journal

Chicago Board

S&P 100 INDEX

Strike	Calls—Last			Puts—Last		
Price	Dec	Jan	Feb	Dec	Jan	Feb
205	33½	...	...	1/16	1/16	...
210	29½	28	...	1/16	⅛	9/16
215	...	23	...	1/16	⅜	13/16
220	19⅞	20⅝	19⅛	1/16	⅝	1 7/16
225	14¾	15½	15¾	3/16	1¼	2 7/16
230	9⅝	11½	13	½	2¼	3¾
235	5	7⅝	9½	1 7/16	4⅛	5½
240	29½	28	...	1/16	⅛	9/16
245	⅞	2⅝	4⅛	1/16	⅝	1 7/16
250	3/16	1½	2⅛	1/16	11¼	1 7/16
255	...	11/16	1 11/16	...	18	...

Total call volume 192,517 Total call open int. 527,341
Total put volume 132,826 Total put open int. 830,472
The index: High 239,26; Low 236,57; Close 238,78 +1,86.

S&P 500 INDEX

Strike	Calls—Last			Puts—Last		
Price	Dec	Jan	Feb	Dec	Jan	Feb
215	...	...	...	...	...	...
220	32	...	...	...	...	...
225	...	...	...	...	¼	...
230	20½	...	22½	1/16	½	1¾
235	17⅛	18	...	3/16	15/16	2⅜
240	11⅜	...	...	⅜	1¾	4
245	6¾	10	12½	1	2⅞	5¾
250	3½	6¼	9⅜	2⅜	4¾	7
255	1⅜	4⅛	7	5¾	7¼	10½
260	⅜	2	...	...	...	...
265	...	...	...	...	19⅛	...

Total call volume 7.522 Total call open int. 105.456
Total put volume 6.963 Total put open int. 86.154
The index: High 251.53; Low 248.94; Close 250.96 +1.68.

American Exchange

MAJOR MARKET INDEX

Strike	Calls—Last			Puts—Last		
Price	Dec	Jan	Feb	Dec	Jan	Feb
315	56	...	...	...	...	...
325	...	...	...	1/16	3/16	...
330	...	...	...	...	3/16	...
335	36	...	...	1/16	½	1
340	...	...	...	1/16	9/16	2⅛
345	26¼	...	...	⅛	1 1/16	2⅞
350	24½	...	...	3/16	1⅝	3⅜
355	20¼	21¾	...	7/16	2 7/16	4⅜

Total call volume 29,3897 Total call open int. 74,279
Total put volume 26,537 Total put open int. 104,052
The index: High 374,35; Low 369,46; Close 373,33 +3,23.

OIL INDEX

Strike	Calls—Last			Puts—Last		
Price	Dec	Jan	Feb	Dec	Jan	Feb
140	...	...	9⅝	...	...	...
145	4	5⅜	...	...	...	...
150	17/16	2¾	...	2½	...	...
155	5/16	1¾	...	...	...	...

Total call volume 300 Total call open int. 3.055
Total put volume 5 Total put open int. 737
The index: High 148.72; Low 146.08; Close 148.33, +2.05.

INSTITUTIONAL INDEX

Strike	Calls—Last			Puts—Last		
Price	Dec	Jan	Feb	Dec	Jan	Feb
225	...	...	...	...	3/16	...
235	20	28	...	...	11/16	...
240	15	...	...	¼	1 5/16	...
245	9⅞	...	...	¾	2¾	...
250	5¼	7⅔	9½	1 3/16	3¾	6¼
255	2¼	...	6½	3	5¾	...
260	11/16	2 9/16	...	6¾	...	...
270	...	...	...	16¾	17⅞	...

Total call volume 5.022 Total call open int. 28.314
Total put volume 1.385 Total put open int. 25.439
The index: High 254.10; Low 251.16; Close 253.58 +2.03.

Philadelphia Exchange

GOLD/SILVER INDEX

Strike	Calls—Last			Puts—Last		
Price	Dec	Jan	Feb	Dec	Jan	Feb
65	12	...	...	...	...	...
70	3	...	...	1/16	⅛	...
75	...	...	...	¾	2 3/16	3¼
80	¾	2½	...	3¼	...	...

Total call volume 151 Total cost open int. 1,809
Total put volume 92 Total put open int. 2.707
The index: High 77.67; Low 76.28; Close 76.70 +0.56.

VALUE LINE INDEX OPTIONS

Strike	Calls—Last			Puts—Last		
Price	Dec	Jan	Feb	Dec	Jan	Feb
215	19¼	...	...	1/16	...	...
220	14¼	...	...	⅛	...	...
225	8½	...	...	⅜	2½	...
230	4	6⅞	...	1⅜	...	...
235	1⅜	3¾	...	4	...	...

Total call volume 1,102 Total call open int. 9,212
Total put volume 412 Total put open int. 6.376
The index: High 231.72; Low 230.54; Close 231.40 +0.58.

NATIONAL O-T-C INDEX

Strike	Calls—Last			Puts—Last		
Price	Dec	Jan	Feb	Dec	Jan	Feb
215	3¼	...	...	...	...	...
220	...	3¾	...	3¾	...	...

Total call volume 151 Total call open int. 1,102
Total put volume 2 Total put open int. 1.264
The index: High 216.10; Low 215.21; Close 215.68 +0.13.

N.Y. Stock Exchange

NYSE INDEX OPTIONS

Strike	Calls—Last			Puts—Last		
Price	Dec	Jan	Feb	Dec	Jan	Feb
125	...	...	...	...	...	¼
130	...	...	...	...	¼	9/16
132½	...	...	...	...	¼	...
135	9¾	...	...	⅛	⅝	1 5/16
137½	...	...	...	3/16	1 1/16	...
140	5	5¾	6¼	½	¼	2¾

Total call volume 5,288 Total call open int. 23,874
Total put volume 4,009 Total put open int. 37.971
The index: High 143.72; Low 142.39; Close 143.46 +0.89.

NYSE BETA INDEX

Strike	Calls—Last			Puts—Last		
Price	Dec	Jan	Feb	Dec	Jan	Feb
290	20¾	...	...	...	...	...
295	15½	...	...	⅜	...	...
300	11¼	...	...	...	...	...
305	8	10¼	...	1 7/16	...	...
310	4¾	7½	...	3¼	7¾	...

Total call volume 124 Total call open int. 947
Total put volume 163 Total put open int. 1,110
The index: High 310.96; Low 306.31; Close 310.15 +1.56.

Pacific Exchange

TECHNOLOGY INDEX

Strike	Calls—Last			Puts—Last		
Price	Dec	Jan	Feb	Dec	Jan	Feb
115	...	...	7¼	2½	...	...

Total call volume 60 Total call open int. 75
Total put volume 102 Total put open int. 33
The index: High 116.56; Low 115.97; Close 116.51 +0.32.

FINANCIAL NEWS COMPOSITE INDEX

Strike	Calls—Last			Puts—Last		
Price	Dec	Jan	Feb	Dec	Jan	Feb
155	20¾	...	...	...	...	...
160	15½	...	...	...	...	...
165	...	...	...	...	1 1/16	...
170	5¾	6¾	...	9/16	2	...
175	2¼	4¼	...	2¼	4¼	...

Total call volume 1,060 Total call open int. 7,658
Total put volume 417 Total put open int. 7,291
The index: High 117.29; Low 173.18; Close 174.85 +1.45.

If the stock market climate is unfavorable, panic selling can be avoided by using index options to protect a portfolio while the investor proceeds with an orderly sell-off.

Index options are particularly useful in separating market risk from stock and industry risk in managing a portfolio. The effects of marketwide movements on a concentrated portfolio may be reduced by hedging in the options market. Index options can be used to change the sensitivity of a portfolio (beta) to market movements.

Index options may be combined or used with other securities to create "synthetic" securities tailor-made for an individual investor's strategy. For example, index options and index futures are a combination that can be very exciting and profitable, albeit risky.

Many different strategies are obviously available to the individual investor using index options. However, before we discuss these strategies, it is vital for the reader to understand how indexes are constructed and some fundamental characteristics of index options.

INDEX CHARACTERISTICS

In general, speculators look for volatile indexes. Portfolio protectors (hedgers), on the other hand, look for the index that best replicates the price movements of their portfolio. A successful strategy incorporating index options depends on accurately identifying the index that is best for a particular technique. So it is necessary to understand the behavior of the underlying index to achieve maximum benefit from index option strategies. This behavior can be defined many ways. The objective, components, construction, and price history of an index are all important in this context.

INDEX VERSUS AVERAGE   Although we refer to them generally as "indexes" there are actually two types of stock market performance indicators used in the United States, indexes and averages. An average is simply the mean value of prices for a group of stock. The Dow Jones Industrial Average (DJIA) is an example. Of the 12 optionable indexes, 3 are actually averages, the Amex Major Market Index, the Amex Transportation Index, and the Pacific Stock Exchange Technology Index.

Stock averages are simple calculations of a group's mean price. In theory, the prices of the stocks are added together and divided by the number of stocks in the group. Exhibit 1-3 shows a simple stock average calculation. The prices of the stocks included are added together and divided by four to give an average of 62.5.

Exhibit 1-3
Stock Price Average

Stock	Price
A	$ 75
B	65
C	60
D	50
Sum	$250
Divisor	4
Average	62.5 (250/4)

In practice, calculating stock averages is complicated by stock splits and stock dividends. For example, if stock D split two-for-one, the value of the average would decline to 56.25 as shown in Exhibit 1-4.

Exhibit 1-4
Stock Average with Stock Split

Stock	Price
A	$ 75
B	65
C	60
D	25
Sum	$225
Divisor	4
Average	56.25 (225/4)

Although the value of stock D to shareholders did not change, the value of the average declined significantly. To correct for this inconsistency, the divisor is adjusted so that the average will not be affected by the split. In this example the divisor would be reduced so that the average would be unaffected by the split of stock D. The new average is determined by adjusting the divisor so that the value after the split equals the average before the split. In our example the divisor is reduced to 3.6, as shown in Exhibit 1-5.

Exhibit 1-5
Stock Average Corrected for Split

Stock	Price
A	$ 75
B	65
C	60
D	25
Sum	$225
Divisor	3.6
Average	62.5 (225/3.6)

Stock averages are further complicated by two additional problems. On occasion, one or more of the stocks in an average may be changed for several reasons. A firm may no longer fit within the sector of the market that the index reflects because of a change in the company's asset base. Or a stock may be removed from an index because of a dramatic deterioration in the company's financial health. The index's advisory board decides to add or delete a company from the index. If a stock is dropped from the index, the divisor must be adjusted.

If a stock's price is much higher or lower than the other stocks included, the average may be distorted by small price changes in the high-priced stock. Conversely, a low-priced stock may change dramatically but have a very small impact on the average. For example, take out a sheet of paper and calculate the average of the stocks listed in Exhibit 1-6. The value of the divisor is five. Now increase the price of stock A by 10 percent to $220 and recalculate the average.

The average increased by 4 percent. Now increase stock E's price by 10 percent to $33. The average increases by a scant .6 percent. In fact, the price of stock E would have to increase by two thirds to match the effect of a 10 percent increase in stock A.

Exhibit 1-6

Stock	Price
A	$200
B	85
C	60
D	1250
E	30

Indexes are a special type of average. The fundamental difference is that indexes are calculated against a benchmark (usually 100) at some point in time (base period) for comparative purposes. An average may be converted to an index by selecting a base period, calculating the value of the average in the base period, and dividing the current average by the base average. Calculation of a hypothetical index is shown in Exhibit 1-7.

Exhibit 1-7
Stock Index Calculation
(base period)

Stock	Price	
A	$75	
B	65	
C	60	
D	50	
Sum	$250	
Divisor	4	
Average	62.5	(250/4)
Index	100.0	(62.5/62.5) * 100 = 100

As the values of the component stocks change, the value of the index is adjusted accordingly. Calculate the value of the index for the stocks listed in Exhibit 1-8. The base period average was 62.5, the index base was 100, and the divisor was four.

Exhibit 1-8

Stock	Price
A	$115
B	64
C	80
D	60

The new index value is 120. The sum of the prices ($300) divided by 4, which equals 75, divided by the base period average (62.5) times the index base (100) gives a new index value of 120. The index is handy because comparisons to the base year are easily observed. The index just calculated increased by 20 percent (from 100 to 120) over the base period. This is seen clearly in the change of the index. The percentage of change in the average from (62.5 to 7's) is less obvious.

Almost all optionable indexes are also weighted in some manner. This value weighting has two key objectives, First, it makes the index sensitive to changes in the market value of the issues involved. Second, it eliminates the effect of stock splits since the stock value (stock price times shares outstanding) remains constant. In a **market-value weighting** scheme, a stock's influence on the average is directly proportional to changes in the stock's market value. Thus, the relative importance of a stock is determined by its total market value relative to the total index market value. A market-value weighted index is calculated in Exhibit 1-9. The price of each stock is multiplied by the number of shares outstanding to determine the stock's market value. The market values of all stocks in the index are added together to yield the market value of the index. The current market value of the index is divided by the market value in the base period to determine the value of the index.

Exhibit 1-9
Market Value Weighted Stock
Index Calculation
(base period)

Stock	Price	Shares	Value
A	$75	1,000,000	75,000,000
B	65	1,500,000	97,500,000
C	60	1,250,000	75,000,000
D	50	2,000,000	100,000,000

Total Market Value $347,500,000

Index = (347,500,000 / 347,500,000) * 100 = 100

There are several advantages to market-value weighted indexes in addition to those cited above. The larger, more important stocks have a greater impact on the value of the index. Also, the divisor does not have to be recalculated as it is with stock averages. Thus, the base value is relatively constant regardless of stock splits, dividends, and conversions.

Calculate the change in the index shown in Exhibit 1-9 with the following changes:

1. Stock A is now selling for $80/share.
2. Stock B is now selling for $55/share.
3. Stock C is now selling at $35/share after a 2-for-1 split.
4. Stock D is now selling at $45/share.

The effect of these changes is shown in Exhibit 1-10. Notice that the *price* of stock C declined dramatically from $60/share to $35/share, but the *market* value of C improved from $75 million to $87.5 million because of the split. As mentioned, adjustment of the divisor is required in an index calculation.

Given this introduction to stock index construction, we can now look at specific optionable indexes.

Exhibit 1-10
Adjusted Stock Index

Stock	Price	Shares	Value
A	$80	1,000,000	80,000,000
B	55	1,500,000	82,500,000
C	35	2,500,000	87,500,000
D	45	2,000,000	90,000,000

Total Market Value $340,000,000

Index = (340,000,000 / 347,500,000) * 100 = 97.84

TRADED INDEX OPTIONS

STANDARD & POOR'S 100 & 500 INDEX Both S & P indexes are constructed using a market-value weighting scheme. The only major difference between the two indexes is their respective size. The S & P 100 represents roughly 40 percent of the market value of the 500 stock index. The value of the stocks in the S & P 500 is roughly 80 percent of the market value of all stocks listed on the New York Stock Exchange. Since 1976, the S & P 500 has included stocks listed on the American Stock Exchange and traded in the over-the-counter market in addition to NYSE listings. Because it is so comprehensive, the S & P 500 has been used as a benchmark for portfolio performance. If your portfolio return is better than the S & P 500, then you "beat the market."

The makeup of the 500 and 100, may be altered over time due to acquisitions, mergers, or a firms financial problems. Also, if a company changes so that it no longer belongs in its industry group, it may be removed. The Standard & Poor's Administrative Committee is responsible for these decisions.

The major investment feature of S & P index options is the broad-based market coverage they provide. This allows managers of well-diversified portfolios to significantly reduce market risk, which they cannot do using traditional investment techniques. Speculators who are predicting marketwide changes in stock prices also use the S&P 100 and 500 index options.

Two narrow-based indexes are offered by Standard & Poor's. The Integrated International Oil Index includes the major Oil & Gas company stocks such as Exxon and Royal Dutch. The Computer & Business Equipment Index includes such giants as IBM and Digital Equipment. Both of these indexes are market-value weighted as well.

AMEX GROUP *Major Market Index*—The major market index (MMI) is a "blue-chip" index that has been used as a surrogate for the Dow Jones Industrial Average (DJIA). The MMI is composed of 20 of the 30 stocks included in the DJIA. The stocks are weighted equally in this index, which is actually a simple average, like the DJIA. The MMI was created because the DJIA is not optionable. The 20 stocks in the MMI are shown in Exhibit 1-11.

Exhibit 1-11
Amex Major Market Index
Component Stocks

American Express	International Paper
AT&T	Johnson & Johnson
Coca Cola	Merck
Dow Chemical	Minnesota Mining & Manu.
duPont	Mobil
Eastman Kodak	Phillip Morris
Exxon	Proctor & Gamble
General Electric	Sears, Roebuck
General Motors	Standard Oil of Calif.
IBM	USX

The MMI is popular with managers of portfolios heavily weighted in blue-chip stocks and speculators who predict price changes in the blue-chip market.

Oil & Gas Index—The Oil & Gas Index (XOI) is a market-value weighted index composed of the 30 leading oil and gas stocks traded in the United States. This narrow-based index is popular with small investors who want to speculate on oil stocks as a group or hedge a portfolio of oil and gas companies. The 30 companies included in this index are shown in Exhibit 1-12.

Exhibit 1-12
Amex Oil & Gas Index
Component Stocks

Amerada Hess	Pennzoil
Apache Corporation	Phillips Petroleum
Atlantic Richfield	Pogo Producing
Diamond Shamrock	Royal Dutch Petroleum
Exxon	Sabine Corporation
Gulf Oil	Shell Oil
Imperial Oil	Standard Oil—Cal.
Inexco Oil	Standard Oil—Ind.
Kerr McGee	Standard Oil—Ohio
Louisiana Land	Sun Company
Mesa Petroleum	Superior Oil
Mitchell Energy	Texaco
Mobil	Texas Oil & Gas
Noble Affiliates	Tosco Corporation
Occidental Petroleum	Unocal Corporation

Computer Technology Index—The Computer Technology Index (XCI) is a market-value weighted index of the 30 largest computer and business information system companies in the United States. As with the Oil and Gas Index, investors can use this index to speculate or hedge on this industry segment. The 30 corporations represented in the XCI are shown in Exhibit 1-13.

NEW YORK STOCK EXCHANGE COMPOSITE INDEX The NYSE Composite Index is a major-value weighted index of all the stocks

---

Exhibit 1-13
Amex Computer Technology Index
Component Stocks

Advanced Micro Devices	Mohawk Data Sciences
Amdahl	Motorola
Automatic Data Processing	National Semiconductor
Burroughs	NBI
Commodore International	NCR
Computer Sciences	Paradyne
Control Data	Prime Computer
Cray Research	Sperry Corporation
Data General	Storage Technology
Datapoint	Tandy
Digital Equipment	Telex
Electronic Data Systems	Texas Instruments
Hewlett-Packard	Tymeshare
Honeywell	Wang Laboratories
IBM	Xerox

---

listed on the New York Stock Exchange. This index does not include stocks listed on other exchanges or those traded over the counter. Managers of portfolios heavily weighted in NYSE stocks rely on this index to manage market risk. Speculators are not particularly fond of this index because it is large and therefore not very volatile. The price history of the NYSE Composite Index is shown in Exhibit 1-14.

Other indexes are also traded on the major options exchanges. Although these are similar to the Indexes outlined previously, they are generally not as popular. One reason for this lack of popularity is that these options are very closely related to the major optionable indexes. Since the major indexes have more trading volume and hence, more liquidity, index option contracts that duplicate the big indexes but are not as liquid will not survive.

Given the characteristics of various major indexes, an obvious question remains: Which index is appropriate for your particular situation? A detailed answer must wait until we discuss speculating and hedging strategies, but we can make a preliminary determination now.

First, take out a piece of paper and list your current holdings. Does this list comprise mostly blue-chip stocks? Then Major Market Index options may be useful in managing your personal portfolio. If you list mostly small, growth-oriented stocks, the Amex Market Value Index may be appropriate for your needs. More than one index may seem to fit your portfolio. List all of these possibilities.

If your portfolio does not seem to conform to any of the indexes listed, perhaps it should be revised. Although streamlining your portfolio may be riskier than you would like, if the new portfolio matches the movements of a major optionable index, the additional risk is manageable. The same logic applies to industry-specific indexes. Instead of owning a little bit of everything and not doing particularly well when gains of some stocks in your portfolio are offset by losses of other stocks, you can concentrate your portfolio a bit more and use index options to offset the potential increase in risk.

INDEX OPTION FUNDAMENTALS

The major features of index options contracts are also listed below.

Contract Value—The total value of a stock index option contract is $100 times the index value. For example, if the S & P 500 index is 230, then the contract value would equal $23,000.

Premium—The option premium may be more relevant than the contract value. Each premium point is equal to $100. Thus, an option with a premium of 3 5/8 would cost $362.50 to purchase (not including transactions expense).

Exercise Prices—Exercise or ''strike'' prices are set at 5 point intervals. New strike prices are introduced as the index level advances and declines.

Cash Settlement—The settlement procedure for an index option is somewhat unusual for the inexperienced investor. All settlements for index option contracts are made in cash. No securities change hands since.

When an investor exercises an index option, he or she is entitled to the difference between the option strike price and the index value at the close of trading on the day of exercise, multiplied by 100 provided the index value is greater than the exercise price (the option is in the money). For example, if you exercise an index call with a strike of 220 and the index value is 230, you receive $1,000.

PROBLEMS & QUESTIONS

1. What is the difference between an average and an index?
2. Why are most indexes weighted?
3. List the major optionable indexes. What are the primary components and objectives of each?

Chapter
Two

SPECULATIVE STRATEGIES

A speculator tries to anticipate changes in the market and make a profit by buying or selling the appropriate securities. The speculator generally takes on substantial risk. No other investment vehicle offers speculators as many alternatives for placing market "bets" as stock index options.

This chapter focuses on practical speculative applications of index options. Each technique is discussed thoroughly with emphasis on risk/return potential and the market conditions most suitable for that strategy. The techniques are divided into two general categories: basic strategies and advanced strategies. Before discussing actual strategy, typical "betting" guidelines are offered to increase your potential for profitable speculating.

SPECULATION PRINCIPLES

Most small investors attempting to speculate in the stock market lose money. Generally, this indicates that speculation is very risky, and that betting on market movements requires a far different strategy from just plain investing.

Speculative investing begins with a "market opinion" a forecast of market movement for the next three months or less. A market opinion can take several forms:

1. *Bullish*—Anticipating a market rise in the near future.
2. *Neutral*—Anticipating small movement of stock prices in the near future.
3. *Major Change, Uncertain Direction*—Anticipating a major move in stock prices, but unsure of the direction.
4. *Bearish*—Anticipating a market decline in the near future.
5. *No Opinion*—No opinion is developed and thus, no position is established (i.e. a stay-out-of-the-market opinion).

Speculators often have more specific expectations. For example, an investor may be *strongly* bullish or *moderately* bearish. These modifications have important strategy implications.

Having the correct market opinion does not always mean investments will be profitable. Market speculation requires discipline. Frequently, inexperienced speculators will hold a winning position too long thinking that "I'm on a roll" only to be disappointed when profits evaporate. Even worse, inexperienced traders may stay with a losing position hoping that it will turn around. Either case virtually guarantees losses in market speculation. A few simple rules should help you avoid these pitfalls:

1. Never speculate when you are optimistic, only when you are confident—Optimism is expecting the best, confidence is knowing you can handle the worst. Only speculate with money you can afford to lose. Nothing is more painful than dipping into your savings or current income to cover a market bet gone sour. The traditional rule of thumb is to limit your speculative position to 10 percent of your investment funds.

2. Make your exit decision before you invest—Establish *realistic* profit goals and loss constraints before entering a position. Once you have established the position, follow your rules! Don't be swept up in the excitement of a winning position or wishful thinking concerning a losing one. Most professional traders establish a specific return as an exit strategy. For example, one trader always liquidates a position when he has a 25 percent return or a 10 percent loss. Both of these limits could be reached quickly if you trade in stock index options.

3. Build in flexibility—Always have more in your speculation account than the minimum required margin. This adds flexibility allowing you to weather the sometimes volatile price movements associated with index options. Many traders hold twice the required margin in their account to give them this flexibility.

4. *You don't have to invest*—Professional traders often have a stay-out-of-the-market opinion. Only assume a position when you have strong feelings about its potential for success. This increases your chances for extracting profits from the market.

5. *Practice before you preach*—Never enter a position without practicing it on paper first. Keep a record of your paper ''gains'' and ''losses'' before you actually invest. If you track a particular strategy, you will see how the position holds up under changing market conditions, how timely your information must be, and whether stop-loss orders should be included, as well as accumulating other information that may be useful. You may also track several positions to compare relative performance. Don't make the mistake of trying to duplicate the winning strategy. That particular strategy was profitable under a specific set of market conditions. Those conditions may not be relevant when you decide to invest. Your goal should be to learn about the dynamics of each position: How rapidly do profits or losses accumulate? Does this position require more timely information? How badly do I lose in this position if I am wrong?

Following these principles will improve your chances of becoming a successful speculator. The next step in the process is to transform your market opinion into a speculative strategy.

BASIC SPECULATIVE STRATEGIES

Regardless of the strategy you choose, certain basic considerations should be included, as outlined in Exhibit 2-1. The format given will be followed as we look at each strategy in detail so that you can quickly compare alternative strategies for any given market opinion.

BUY (LONG) CALL OPTIONS   Exhibit 2-2 summarizes the strategy of buying call options. There is no margin requirement since the options are paid for in full at purchase. If you want to place a market bet, then this is the easiest strategy to implement. If the market rises, you win. If the market falls, you lose. The risk is limited to the initial

---

Exhibit 2-1
Standard Stragegy for Index Options

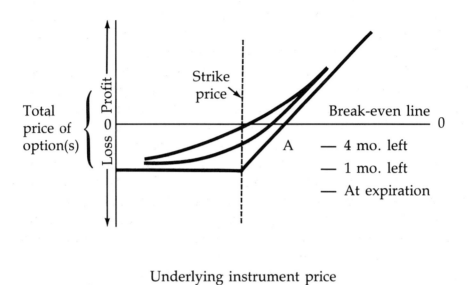

SITUATION: A one-sentence description of anticipated market activity.

OBJECTIVE: A one-sentence description of how the investor can profit from the anticipated situation.

STRATEGY: The specific action taken by the investor.

ANALYSIS: Comments on index and option selection.

RISK/RETURN: A comment on the risk/return profile for this strategy.

EXAMPLES:
A few examples of implementing the strategy with possible outcomes.

premium paid or 100 percent of your bet, and the profit potential is unlimited.

Exhibit 2-2
Buy Call Options

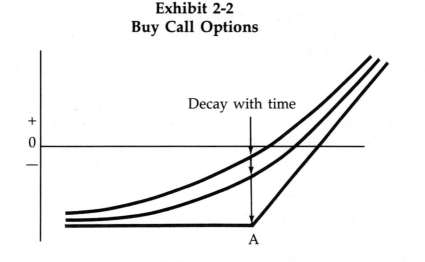

SITUATION: Anticipate strong marketwide or segment advance.

OJECTIVE: To profit from sharp increase in index value.

STRATEGY: Buy stock index call options.

ANALYSIS: Identify the particular index you think will rise. Highest potential return involves purchasing out-of-the-money options. Lower expected returns and risk can be achieved by purchasing in-the-money options.

RISK/RETURN: If anticipated advance fails to materialize, 100% of your investment could be lost. Also, options are decaying investments, that is, the value of your investment declines over time as expiration approaches.

EXAMPLES:
Buy one S&P 500 220 call at 4.00 on October 5   (Index = 220)
Sell S&P 500 220 call at 7.25 on October 21   (Index = 225)
Profit = 7.25 − 4.00 = 3.25 × 100 = $325.00 on $400 investment.

Buy one S&P 500 220 call at 4.00 on October 5   (Index = 220)
Call expires worthless in November   (Index = 210)
Loss = 4.00 × 100 = $400.00 on $400 investment.

The actual index option selected depends on your opinion. If you forecast a strong general market rise, then buy a broad-market call option like the S&P 500. If you predict a strong rise in a narrow segment, like blue-chip securities, then buy a Major Market Index call option.

After identifying the index, you must decide which call option to purchase. Selecting an out-of-the-money call option (strike price is greater than current index value) requires less capital, but the option is worthless at expiration if the index value does not increase beyond the option strike price. This means a 100 percent loss of capital. Purchasing in-the-money options (strike price is less than current index value) requires more capital without a significant reduction in risk. Therefore, the recommended purchase is an out-of-the-money option.

BUY PUT OPTIONS Put options are purchased to profit from market declines. Exhibit 2-3 describes this strategy. If the index declines significantly before expiration, you will profit. If the index stays the same or rises, the put option premium will fall. The method for selecting the index and option is identical to the process described for buying calls. (Puts are out of the money if the strike price is less than the index value.)

SELL (SHORT) CALL OPTIONS If you are mildly bearish to neutral about the market or a particular segment, selling call options, (see Exhibit 2-4) is an appropriate strategy. This is a high-risk strategy, however, since your profit potential is limited to the premium received when the option is sold, but risk is unlimited.

Assume that you expect the market to stay the same or decline slightly over the next few months. You sell an at-the-money S&P 500 call option with a strike price of 220 for a premium of $350 per option. If the index value stays the same or declines by expiration, you gain the entire $350 per option. This is your maximum profit. However, if the index increases, you have unlimited liability for the difference between the index value and the strike price. If the index value at expiration is between 220 and 223.5 (remember each point is equal to $100) you will forfeit some or all of the $350 premium income you received when you entered the position. If the index value is more than 223.5 at expiration, you must pay the difference. The risk is theoretically unlimited. Therefore, this strategy should only be

---

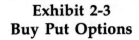

Exhibit 2-3
Buy Put Options

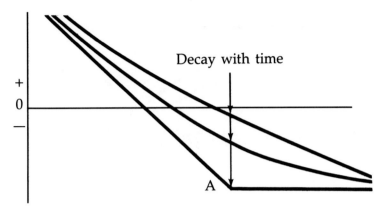

SITUATION: Anticipate strong marketwide or segment decline.

OBJECTIVE: To profit from a sharp decline in index value.

STRATEGY: Buy stock index put options.

ANALYSIS: Identify the particular index you think will decline. Highest return potential involves purchasing out-of-the-money options. Lower expected returns and risk can be achieved by purchasing in-the-money options.

RISK/RETURN: If anticipated decline fails to materialize, 100% of your investment could be lost. Also, options are decaying investments, that is, the value of your investment declines over time as expiration approaches.

EXAMPLES:
Buy one S&P 500 220 put at 4.00 on October 5   (Index = 220)
Sell S&P 500 220 put at 7.25 on October 21   (Index = 215)
Profit = 7.25 − 4.00 = 3.25 × 100 = $325.00 on $400 investment.

Buy one S&P 500 220 put at 4.00 on October 5   (Index = 220)
Call expires worthless in November   (Index = 225)
Loss = 4.00 × 100 = $400.00 on $400 investment.

Exhibit 2-4
Sell Call Options

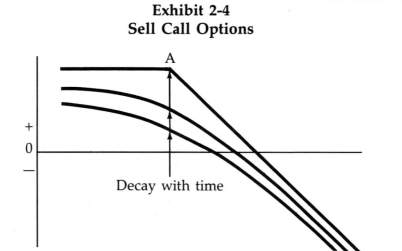

SITUATION: Anticipate neutral market or mild decline.

OBJECTIVE: To gain premium income from market inactivity.

STRATEGY: Sell stock index call options.

ANALYSIS: Identify the particular index you anticipate remaining unchanged. Highest return potential involves selling in-the-money options. Lower expected returns and risk can be achieved by selling out-of-the-money options.

RISK/RETURN: Very risky strategy. Profit potential limited to premium received. If index should rise sharply, your loss is theoretically unlimited.

EXAMPLES:
Sell one S&P 500 220 call at 4.00 on October 5   (Index = 220)
S&P 500 220 call expires worthless in November   (Index = 218)
Profit = 4.00 × 100 = $400.00.

Sell one S&P 500 220 call at 4.00 on October 5   (Index = 220)
Buy S&P 500 220 call at 8.00 on October 21 (Index = 226)
Loss = 4.00 × 100 = $400.00.

---

considered if you tell your broker to close out your position when the index value exceeds a certain limit to prevent excessive losses.

SELL PUT OPTIONS If you expect the market to rise slightly or stay the same selling put options is an acceptable strategy. This strategy is subject to the same risks as selling call options. Risk is unlimited while profits are limited to the premium income. The specifics of selling put options are outlined in Exhibit 2-5.

As with selling calls, this strategy takes advantage of the fact that index options are a decaying asset in that the value declines over time. Sellers (writers) of options reap the benefits of the decay.

As a result, option writers want no price movement, or at worst slight movement in the anticipated direction. In contrast, option buyers not only want price movement in the anticipated direction, but they want it quickly.

BUY STRADDLE A straddle is a combination of a put and a call option with the same exercise price and expiration date; for example, buy a March SPX (S&P 500) 220 call and buy a March SPX 220 put. This strategy is used when you expect a major market move but are uncertain about the direction. Exhibit 2-6 summarizes the key items in this strategy.

Buying straddles is less risky than buying only a call or a put. Your prediction is that the market will move quickly, but not the direction. Many traders use this strategy when they see the volatility of the market increasing. The weakness of this strategy is that the value of the straddle decays as expiration approaches. The decay effect is most obvious in the month before expiration. Consequently, purchasing straddles with maturities of less than six to eight weeks is not recommended.

Deciding when to remove a straddle is difficult. If you correctly anticipated a major change in the market, then the value of your straddle has increased, but this value decays with time. Some traders exit the straddle position by "rolling up" or "rolling down." For example, you purchase an SPX 220 straddle with four months to expiration. If the index value moves, you can sell your 220 straddle and reposition around the current index value. This can be repeated as long as you expect major changes in the value of an index, but are uncertain about the direction.

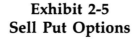

Exhibit 2-5
Sell Put Options

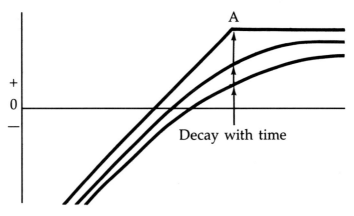

SITUATION: Anticipate neutral market or mild rise.

OBJECTIVE: To gain premium income from market inactivity.

STRATEGY: Sell stock index put options.

ANALYSIS: Identify the particular index you anticipate remaining unchanged. Highest return potential involves selling in-the-money options. Lower expected returns and risk can be achieved by selling out-of-the-money options.

RISK/RETURN: Very risky strategy. Profit potential limited to premium received. If index should decline sharply, your loss is theoretically unlimited.

EXAMPLES:
Sell one S&P 500 220 put at 4.00 on October 5   (Index = 220)
S&P 500 220 put expires worthless in November   (Index = 223)
Profit = 4.00 × 100 = $400.00.

Sell one S&P 500 220 put at 4.00 on October 5   (Index = 220)
Buy S&P 500 220 put at 8.00 on October 21   (Index = 214)
Loss = 4.00 × 100 = $400.00.

Exhibit 2-6
Buy Index Option Straddle

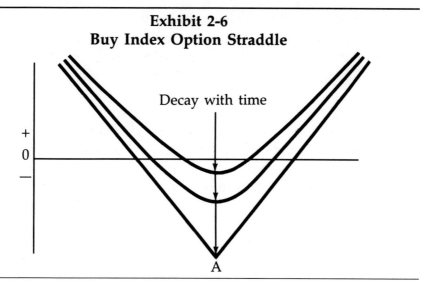

SITUATION: Anticipate major market movement, uncertain direction.

OBJECTIVE: To profit from significant change in index value.

STRATEGY: Buy put and call with same exercise price and maturity.

ANALYSIS: Identify the particular index you anticipate changing. Highest return potential involves setting the straddle strike price equal to the current index value.

RISK/RETURN: This is less risky than buying either only calls and puts. Primary risk is decay of investment as expiration of straddle approaches.

EXAMPLES:
Buy one S&P 500 220 call at 4.00 on October 5   (Index = 220)
Buy one S&P 500 220 put at 3.75 on October 5

Sell S&P 500 220 call at 8.00 on October 21   (Index = 226)
Sell S&P 500 220 put at 1.75 on October 21

Profit = 9.75 − 7.75 = 2.00 × 100 = $200.00 on $775 investment

Buy one S&P 500 220 call at 4.00 on October 5   (Index = 220)
Buy one S&P 500 220 put at 3.75 on October 5

Both options expire worthless in November   (Index = 220)

Loss = 7.75 × 100 = $775 investment.

The break-even position in a straddle purchase is equal to the index value plus the total premium paid for the two options. For example, if you paid a total premium of $650 per option (6.5 points) and the straddle was set at 220, you would profit if the index value exceeded 226.5 or was less than 213.5 at expiration.

SELL A STRADDLE   If you anticipate little movement in the market, selling an index option straddle can be a profitable strategy. Exhibit 2-7 outlines the basics of this strategy. The objective is to benefit from the decaying value of the index options.

Profit is limited to the premium income received when the position is established. The break-even position in a sell straddle is equal to the index value plus the total premium for the two options. If you received a total premium of $650 per option (6.5 points) and the straddle was set at 220, you would profit if the index value was between 226.5 and 213.5 at expiration. Your risk is unlimited if the index value moves above or below the straddle strike price plus the amount of premium received. If the index value changes substantially before expiration, you can roll up or roll down the straddle to limit your risk as described in the section on buying straddles.

Since the objective in selling straddle is to gain value from decaying option premiums, this strategy should be used when that decay is the greatest, near expiration. However, this is also when risk is greatest for a straddle writer, so stop-loss orders should be used.

BUY STRANGLE AND SELL STRANGLE   These strategies are identical to buying and selling straddles buying except that the strike prices for the puts and calls are different. Exhibits 2-8 and 2-9 explain these strategies in detail. Usually, the options purchased or sold are out of the money. This reduces cost, risk, and profit potential relative to the straddle technique. Therefore, strangles are a less risky alternative to straddles given the same market opinion.

These eight strategies provide you with techniques to take advantage of many market opinions. If you are strongly bullish, buying call options is a good strategy. Put options may be purchased if you are strongly bearish. If your opinion is less strong, selling index calls or puts would be appropriate if you are moderately bearish or bullish, respectively. If you anticipate a major move, but feel uncomfortable

---

Exhibit 2-7
Sell Index Option Straddle

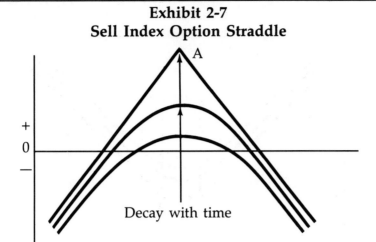

Decay with time

SITUATION: Anticipate no market movement.

OBJECTIVE: To gain premium income during market inactivity.

STRATEGY: Sell put and call with same exercise price and maturity.

ANALYSIS: Identify the particular index you anticipate remaining unchanged. Highest return potential involves setting the straddle strike price equal to the current index value.

RISK/RETURN: Profit is limited to premium income received when straddle is established. Risk is unlimited if index changes dramatically.

EXAMPLES:
Sell one S&P 500 220 call at 4.00 on October 5   (Index = 220)
Sell one S&P 500 220 put at 3.75 on October 5

Both options expire worthless in November   (Index = 220)

Profit = 7.75 × 100 = $775.00.

Sell one S&P 500 220 call at 4.00 on October 5   (Index = 220)
Sell one S&P 500 220 put at 3.75 on October 5

Buy S&P 500 220 call at 8.00 on October 21   (Index = 226)
Buy S&P 500 220 put at 1.75 on October 21

Loss = 7.75 − 9.75 = −2.00 × 100 = −$200.00 on $775 investment

---

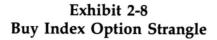

Exhibit 2-8
Buy Index Option Strangle

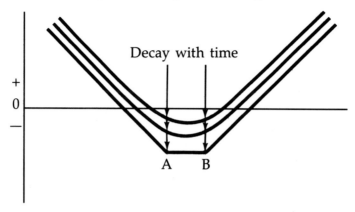

SITUATION: Anticipate major market movement, uncertain direction.

OBJECTIVE: To profit from significant change in index value.

STRATEGY: Buy put and call with different exercise price but same maturity.

ANALYSIS: Identify the particular index you anticipate changing. Highest potential return involves setting the strangle strike price close to the current index value.

RISK/RETURN: Less risky than buying a straddle. Primary risk is decay of investment as expiration of straddle approaches.

EXAMPLES:
Buy one S&P 500 225 call at 2.00 on October 5   (Index = 220)
Buy one S&P 500 215 put at 1.75 on October 5

Sell S&P 500 225 call at 4.00 on October 21   (Index = 226)
Sell S&P 500 215 put at 0.75 on October 21

Profit = 4.75 − 3.75 = 1.00 × 100 = $100.00 on $375 investment

Buy one S&P 500 225 call at 2.00 on October 5   (Index = 220)
Buy one S&P 500 215 put at 1.75 on October 5

Both options expire worthless in November (Index = 220)

Loss = 3.75 × 100 = $375 investment.

Exhibit 2-9
Sell Index Option Strangle

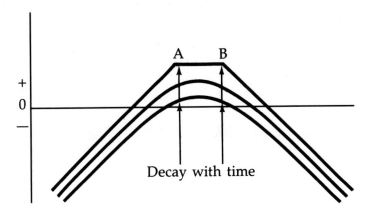

SITUATION: Anticipate no market movement.

OBJECTIVE: To gain premium income during market inactivity.

STRATEGY: Sell put and call with different exercise price but same maturity.

ANALYSIS: Identify the particular index you anticipate remaining unchanged. Highest potential return involves setting the strangle strike prices close to the current index value.

RISK/RETURN: Profit is limited to premium income received when strangle is established. Risk is unlimited if index changes dramatically.

EXAMPLES:
Sell one S&P 500 225 call at 2.00 on October 5   (Index = 220)
Sell one S&P 500 215 put at 1.75 on October 5

Both options expire worthless in November   (Index = 220)

Profit = 3.75 × 100 = $375.00.

Sell one S&P 500 225 call at 2.00 on October 5   (Index = 220)
Sell one S&P 500 215 put at 1.75 on October 5

Buy S&P 500 225 call at 4.00 on October 21   (Index = 226)
Buy S&P 500 215 put at 0.75 on October 21

Loss = 4.75 − 3.75 = −1.00 × 100 = −$100.00 on $375 investment

predicting the direction, buy straddles or strangles. If you anticipate a stable market, selling straddles or strangles may be profitable.

These basic strategies allow you to easily and quickly convert a
market opinion into a speculative investment action. In the next section we will look at more advanced strategies. These strategies are
considered "advanced" only because they require either more
research or more timely information. Otherwise, the techniques are
easy to follow and apply.

ADVANCED SPECULATIVE STRATEGIES

Advanced trading strategies are meant to optimize gains while reducing the risks associated with the basic strategies. The most common
of these strategies is the **spread**. Two basic types of spread are used
in the market. The **vertical option spread** involves buying and selling two options with different strike prices. Buying and selling two
options with different expiration dates is a **horizontal spread**.

Buying any option involves a payment (debit) while selling an
option means a payment (credit) is received. As a result, your
account will either have a debit or credit balance when you initiate
a spread. If you pay more for an option than you receive from the
sale of another option, your account will have a debit balance. If
you receive more for selling an option than you pay for buying
an option, your account has a credit balance. Although this may
seem fairly obvious, it can have a significant effect if you trade in
spreads.

VERTICAL SPREADS   Many types of vertical spreads are available to the speculator. The four most common are the **call/debit**,
the **call/credit**, the **put/debit**, and the **put/credit**.

Call/Debit Spread—A vertical call/debit spread involves buying an
index call option with a low strike price (a high premium) and simultaneously selling an identical index call option with a higher strike
price (a low premium). The total value of your account will be equal
to the low premium minus the high premium, or a debit balance
(net premium paid).

For example, suppose option prices were as follows:

Index	Index Value	Maturity	Strike Price	Premium
SPX	235.48	Oct.	Call 240	11/16
SPX	235.48	Oct.	Call 235	2 9/16

Assuming that a vertical call/debit spread would involve buying the 235 strike option for $256.25 (2 9/16 × $100) and selling the 240 strike option for $68.75 (11/16 × $100). The total cost of the spread is $187.50 ($256.25 – 68.75). Now suppose that the index value increased to 240.5 under the following conditions:

Index	Index Value	Maturity	Strike Price	Premium
SPX	240.00	Oct.	Call 240	3 2/16
SPX	240.00	Oct.	Call 235	8 13/16

The new value of the spread would be equal to $881.25 (8 13/16 × $100) minus $312.50 (3 2/16 × $100) or $453.25. If you sell the 235 strike option and buy back the 240 option for a net of $453.25, your profit would be $265.75 ($453.25 – 187.5). Comparing this strategy to buying only the 235 strike call option reveals the primary characteristics of a spread. If the 235 option were purchased, total profit under the same circumstances would have been higher, $625.00 ($881.25 – $256.25). However, if the index value had declined, only $187.50 would be risked by initiating the spread as opposed to the full $256.25. The vertical call/debit spread would be used if you expect a bull market. Index calls would also be purchased under the same conditions, but the spread involves less risk (and lower profit potential). The call/debit spread is described in Exhibit 2-10.

Call/Credit Spread—The vertical call/credit spread is used when you think the index won't move much or will decline slightly. The spread involves buying a high strike index call option (paying a low

Exhibit 2-10
Vertical Call/Debit Spread

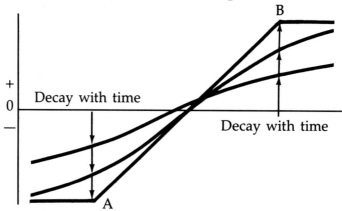

SITUATION: Anticipate moderate index rise.

OBJECTIVE: To profit from moderate rise in index value.

STRATEGY: Buy an index call with a low strike price (a high premium) and simultaneously sell an identical index call option with a higher strike price (a low premium).

ANALYSIS: Identify the particular index you anticipate rising. The call/debit spread is less risky than purchasing only call options alone.

RISK/RETURN: If the index level doesn't rise, less of your investment is risked when compared to a straight call purchase. However, the return on the spread is lower than the return from a straight call if the index does rise.

EXAMPLES:

Buy one S&P 500 235 call at $2.5625 on October 5   (Index = 235)
Sell one S&P 500 240 call at $0.6875 on October 5

Both options expire worthless in November   (Index = 220)

Loss = ($2.5625 – $0.6875) × 100 = $187.50

Buy one S&P 500 235 call at $2.5625 on October 5   (Index = 235)
Sell one S&P 500 240 call at $0.6875 on October 5

Sell S&P 500 235 call at $8.8125 on October 21   (Index = 240)
Buy S&P 500 240 call at $3.125 on October 21

Profit = ($8.8125 – $3.125) × 100 = $453.25 – $187.50 = $265.75

premium) and selling an identical option with a lower strike price (receiving a high premium), giving you a credit balance. To illustrate how this works, suppose the following conditions held:

Index	Index Value	Maturity	Strike Price	Premium
SPX	235.48	Oct.	Call 240	11/16
SPX	235.48	Oct.	Call 235	2 9/16

Establishing a call/credit position would involve buying the 240 strike option for $68.25 and selling the 235 option for $256.25. The net balance in your account would be a $187.50 credit. If the index value is 235 or below at expiration in October, then the full $187.50 is profit. If the index value rises, you have the right to buy at 240 and you have sold the right to buy at 235. This $500 (240 – 235 × $100) minus the initial credit of the spread $187.50, or $323.50 ($500 – 187.50) is the most you can lose since no matter how high the index value rises, you have the right to buy at 240. If the index equaled 245, at expiration you would be liable for $1,000 on the 235 option you sold. You would receive $500 on the 240 option you purchased. This $500 loss would be offset by the net premium received when the spread was established, $187.50. Thus, the total loss would be $323.50.

This spread is the less risky alternative to selling call options. Profit potential is lower, but risk is constrained by the higher strike option. Exhibit 2-11 outlines this strategy in detail.

Put/Debit Spread—The vertical put/debit spread is the less risky alternative to buying only put options. A high-strike put option is purchased (for a high premium) while an identical put with a lower strike price is simultaneously purchased (for a low premium). The net premium paid equals the debit balance of your account. For example, suppose the following pertained:

Index	Index Value	Maturity	Strike Price	Premium
SPX	235.48	Oct.	Put 235	2 5/8
SPX	235.48	Oct.	Put 230	1

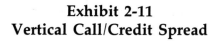

Exhibit 2-11
Vertical Call/Credit Spread

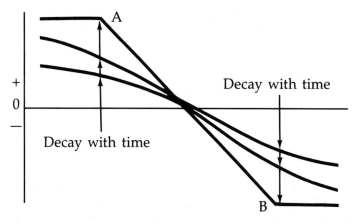

SITUATION: Anticipate little movement or slight decline in index.

OBJECTIVE: To gain premium income from small decline in index.

STRATEGY: Buy an index call with a high strike price (a low premium) and simultaneously sell an identical index call option with a lower strike price (a high premium).

ANALYSIS: Identify the particular index you anticipate declining. The call/credit spread is less risky than selling call options alone.

RISK/RETURN: If the index level doesn't decline, less of your investment is risked when compared to a straight call sale. However, the return on the spread is lower than a straight call sale if the index value does decline.

EXAMPLES:

Sell one S&P 500 235 call at $2.5625 on October 5   (Index = 235)
Buy one S&P 500 240 call at $0.6875 on October 5

Both options expire worthless in November   (Index = 220)

Profit = ($2.5625 – $0.6875) × 100 = $187.50

Buy one S&P 500 240 call at $0.6875 on October 5   (Index = 235)
Sell one S&P 500 235 call at $2.5625 on October 5

Buy S&P 500 235 call at $8.8125 on October 21   (Index = 240)
Sell S&P 500 240 call at $3.125 on October 21

Loss = ($8.8125¹$3.125) × 100 = –$453.25 + $187.50 = –$265.75

The 235 put would be purchased for $262.50 and the 230 put would be sold for $100. The account balance would equal $162.50 ($262.50 − $100) net premium paid (debit). If the index value rises or stays the same, both options would expire worthless. Therefore, the total risk of this spread is the initial cost of $162.50. If the index value falls below 230, say to 225, the maximum profit at expiration would equal the $1,000 received on the 235 put, minus the $500 paid to the holder of the 230 put you wrote, and the initial cost of the spread, $162.5, or a total of $337.50. If you expect the index to decline, this spread can be used in lieu of the more risky alternative, purchasing put options alone. Exhibit 2-12 summarizes this strategy.

Put/Credit Spread—If you are moderately bullish or neutral about the future value of an index, the vertical put/credit spread is a good strategy. Using the situation outlined in the previous example, we can examine this technique in detail:

Index	Index Value	Maturity	Strike Price	Premium
SPX	235.48	Oct.	Put 235	2 5/8
SPX	235.48	Oct.	Put 230	1

With a put/credit spread the high strike option (235) is sold and $262.50 is credited to your account. Simultaneously, the low strike (230) option is purchased, resulting in a reduction of your account by $100. The net balance is a $162.50 credit. If the index value is greater than or equal to 235 at expiration, the entire $162.50 is profit since both options expire worthless. If the index value is less than 235, say 230, at expiration, the maximum loss is the $500 paid to the holder of the 235 option (your 230 option expires worthless) minus the initial credit ($162.50), or $327.50. The vertical put/credit spread is less risky than selling only index put options. Exhibit 2-13 outlines this technique.

HORIZONTAL SPREADS   In general, horizontal spreads involve buying and selling two options that are identical except for their maturity date. This technique attempts to benefit from the decaying values of index options. The two primary horizontal spreads are the call/debit and the put/debit.

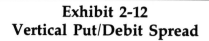

Exhibit 2-12
Vertical Put/Debit Spread

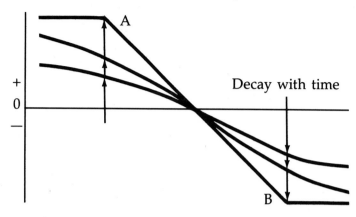

SITUATION: Anticipate moderate index decline.

OBJECTIVE: To profit from moderate decline in index value.

STRATEGY: Buy an index put with a high strike price (a high premium) and simultaneously sell an identical index put option with a lower strike price (a low premium).

ANALYSIS: Identify the particular index you anticipate declining. The put/debit spread is less risky than purchasing put options alone.

RISK/RETURN: If the index doesn't decline, less of your investment is risked when compared to a straight put purchase. However, the return on the spread is lower than a straight put purchase if the index value does rise.

EXAMPLES:

Buy one S&P 500 240 put at $2.5625 on October 5   (Index = 240)
Sell one S&P 500 235 put at $0.6875 on October 5

Both options expire worthless in November   (Index = 245)

Loss = (−$2.5625+$0.6875) × 100 = -$187.50

Buy one S&P 500 240 put at $2.5625 on October 5   (Index = 240)
Sell one S&P 500 235 put at $0.6875 on October 5

Sell S&P 500 240 put at $8.8125 on October 21   (Index = 230)
Buy S&P 500 235 put at $3.125 on October 21

Profit = ($8.8125−$3.125) × 100 = $453.25 − $187.50 = $265.75

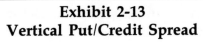

Exhibit 2-13
Vertical Put/Credit Spread

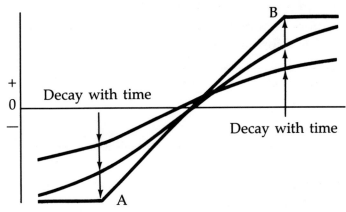

SITUATION: Anticipate moderate index rise.

OBJECTIVE: To profit from moderate rise in index value.

STRATEGY: Buy an index put with a low strike price (a low premium) and simultaneously sell an identical index put option with a higher strike price (a high premium).

ANALYSIS: Identify the particular index you anticipate rising. The put/credit spread is the less risky alternative to selling put options alone.

RISK/RETURN: If the index level doesn't rise, less of your investment is subject to risk when compared to a straight put sale. However, the return on the spread is lower than a straight put sale if the index value does rise.

EXAMPLES:

Sell one S&P 500 240 put at $2.5625 on October 5   (Index = 240)
Buy one S&P 500 235 put at $0.6875 on October 5

Both options expire worthless in November   (Index = 245)

Profit = ($2.5625 – $0.6875) × 100 = $187.50

Sell one S&P 500 240 put at $2.5625 on October 5   (Index = 240)
Buy one S&P 500 235 put at $0.6875 on October 5

Buy S&P 500 240 put at $8.8125 on October 21   (Index = 230)
Sell S&P 500 235 put at $3.125 on October 21

Loss = (– $8.8125 + $3.125) × 100 = – $453.25 + $187.50 = – $265.75

Call/Debit Spread—In a horizontal call/debit spread an index call option is sold and an identical option with a longer maturity is purchased. This spread would be used if you expect the index value to stay the same or rise in the short-run. Since longer maturity options are more expensive, your account will have a debit balance.

Consider the information listed below:

Index	Index Value	Maturity	Strike Price	Premium
SPX	235.48	Oct.	Call 235	2 9/16
SPX	235.48	Nov.	Call 235	6

In this example, the November option is purchased for $600 and the October option is sold for $256.25, leaving your account with a $343.75 debit balance before commissions. You will make a profit because value of the near-term option decays faster than the longer-term option. You are trying to capture the $256.25 premium on the shorter-term option.

The longer-term option will also decline in value, but hopefully not as much as the near-term option. If the index value decreases dramatically, the decline in the November option could exceed the premium received from the October option. However, this risk is limited to the difference between the premium paid ($600) and the premium received ($256.25), or $343.75. If the index stayed the same or rose, the risk of selling the call would be eliminated because you have an identical strike option.

Suppose the index value increased to 240 at the October expiration and the following prices prevailed:

Index	Index Value	Maturity	Strike Price	Premium
SPX	240.00	Oct.	Call 235	5
SPX	240.00	Nov.	Call 235	11 3/8

Notice that the value of the October call is equal to the difference between the strike price (235) and the index value (240). The October call would be exercised for $500. You would meet this requirement by selling the November call for $1,137.50. The difference is equal to $637.50 and your profit would equal $637.50 minus the initial cost of the spread ($343.75), or $256.25.

This strategy is a technique for accruing time value with limited risk. It should be applied when you expect the index value to stay the same or rise. If the index value falls your risk is limited to the initial cost of the spread plus the premium on the long maturity option when the short-term option expires since both options have the same strike price. Exhibit 2-14 outlines this strategy.

Exhibit 2-14
Horizontal Call/Debit Spread

SITUATION: Anticipate little or moderate index increase.

OBJECTIVE: To gain premium income from decay of short maturity option.

STRATEGY: Sell an index call and simultaneously buy an identical index call option with longer maturity.

ANALYSIS: Identify the particular index you anticipate rising. The horizontal call/debit spread profits from the rapid decay of the near-term option you sold and the less rapid decay of the option you purchased.

RISK/RETURN: If the index declines dramatically, losses from the longer-term option may exceed the profit on the near term option. However, this loss is limited to the difference between the premium paid and the premium received.

EXAMPLE:
Sell one S&P 500 Oct. 235 call at $2.5625 on October 5
Buy one S&P 500 Nov. 235 call at $6.00 on October 5

Index value = increases from 235 to 240 at October expiration.

Buy S&P 500 Oct. 235 call at $5.00
Sell S&P 500 Nov. 235 call at $11.375

Profit = ($11.375 − $5.00) × 100 = $637.5 − $343.75 (cost) = $256.25

Put/Debit Spread—The horizontal put/debit spread is used when you are bearish to neutral about the value of a particular index in the near future. Consider the following information:

Index	Index Value	Maturity	Strike Price	Premium
SPX	235.48	Oct.	Put 235	2 5/8
SPX	235.48	Nov.	Put 235	6 1/2

By selling the October put for $262.50 and simultaneously buying the November put for $650, you can establish a put/debit spread. Your account will have a $387.50 debit balance. If the index value rises dramatically, both options will decline in value. However, the most you can lose is $387.50. Practically, the November option should have some value when your October option expires, therefore your loss would be smaller.

If the index declines, both options benefit. The October option, however, will lose more time value than the November option. Therefore, this difference accrues to you as profit. This is shown using the following information:

Index	Index Value	Maturity	Strike Price	Premium
SPX	230.00	Oct.	Put 235	5
SPX	230.00	Nov.	Put 235	11 9/16

The index value has declined to 230. Both option prices have increased, yet the October price represents all intrinsic value. The November price includes both intrinsic value and time value. The difference in prices, $656.25 (1156.25 - $500), is the gain and $268.75 ($656.25 - $387.50; the gain minus the initial cost) is the profit. Exhibit 2-15 outlines this technique in detail.

BUTTERFLY SPREADS   The final speculative strategy we will consider is the butterfly spread, which involves four options, two puts and two calls. This spread can be very profitable while the risk is minimal. Depending on whether you forecast minimal or major market movement, a butterfly spread may be long or short.

Exhibit 2-15
Horizontal Put/Debit Spread

SITUATION: Anticipate little or moderate index decline.

OBJECTIVE: To gain premium income from decay of short maturity option.

STRATEGY: Sell an index put and simultaneously buy an identical index put option with more time until maturity.

ANALYSIS: Identify the particular index you anticipate declining. The horizontal put/debit spread profits from the rapid decay of the near term option you sold and the less rapid decay of the option you purchased.

RISK/RETURN: If the index increases dramatically, losses from the longer-term option may exceed the profit on the near-term option. However, this loss is limited to the difference between the premium paid and the premium received.

EXAMPLE:
Sell one S&P 500 Oct. 235 put at $2.625 on October 5
Buy one S&P 500 Nov. 235 put at $6.50 on October 5

Index value = decreases from 235 to 230 at October expiration.

Buy S&P 500 Oct. 235 put at $5.00
Sell S&P 500 Nov. 235 put at $11.5625

Profit = ($11.5625 − $5.00) × 100 = $656.25 − $387.50 (cost) = $268.75

Long Butterfly—In this technique, the index call options bought and sold are identical except for their strike prices. One call is purchased at the lowest strike price, two calls are purchased at the middle strike price, and one call is purchased at the highest strike price.

Consider the following information:

Index	Index Value	Maturity	Strike Price	Premium
SPX	235.48	Oct.	Call 240	11/16
SPX	235.48	Oct.	Call 235	2 9/16
SPX	235.48	Oct.	Call 230	6 1/8

Two index calls are purchased, the 240 strike and the 230 strike, for $681.25. Two calls are sold, both with a strike of 235, for $512.50. The net debit balance in your account is $168.75. If the index value is 235 at expiration, the following prices will prevail:

Index	Index Value	Maturity	Strike Price	Premium
SPX	235.00	Oct.	Call 240	0
SPX	235.00	Oct.	Call 235	0
SPX	235.00	Oct.	Call 230	5

Exercising your 230 strike option yields $500, which means your total profit is $500 minus the initial cost of the position, $168.75, or $331.25.

If the index value is 240, the 240 strike option expires worthless, you owe $500 each for the 235 calls you sold, and the 230 call is worth $1,000. These values cancel each other out, so your net loss is equal to the initial cost of the spread. This is also true if the index value is more than 240.

If the index value is 230 or below at expiration, all options expire worthless and your loss is limited to the initial $168.75 cost of the spread. If the index is 240 or higher at expiration, the premiums on all of the options cancel each other out and your net loss equals the initial cost of the spread. For example, if the index is 250 at expiration, the 230 option you purchased is worth $2,000. The 235 options you sold are worth $1,500 each or $3,000 total. The 240 option you purchased is worth $1,000, so the net value of your account is $0.00. Your loss is equal to the debit balance when the spread was initiated.

You would obtain maximum profit from the long butterfly when the index value equals the middle strike price at expiration ($331.25

in the example above). Both options you sold expire worthless and the 230 option you purchased is worth $500, which minus the cost of the spread, ($168.75), gives you a profit of $331.25. Therefore, this is a profitable strategy when you expect little movement in the index in the near future. Exhibit 2-16 outlines the details of this technique.

Short Butterfly—If you expect a major move in an index value, the short butterfly can be a good technique. This strategy involves selling an index call option at the lowest strike price, buying two call options at the middle strike price, and selling another call option at the highest strike price.

Suppose the following information pertained:

Index	Index Value	Maturity	Strike Price	Premium
SPX	235.48	Oct.	Call 240	11/16
SPX	235.48	Oct.	Call 235	2 9/16
SPX	235.48	Oct.	Call 230	6 1/8

Selling the 240 and 230 call options yields $681.25 in premium income. Buying two of the 235 call options costs $512.50. Your account will have a $168.75 credit balance. If the index value equals 235 at expiration, the 230 option will be worth $500. All others are worthless. Since you sold this option, you will have to pay $500 to the option holder. Your total loss equals $331.25 ($168.75 − $500). This is the maximum loss from this position.

If the index value was 240 or more or 230 or less, the premiums on the four options would cancel out and you would keep the $168.75 as profit. Suppose the index level at expiration was 245. You would owe $1,500 on the 230 option and $500 on the 240 option. You would receive $2,000 on the two 235 options you purchased. Thus, the total value of your account at expiration would equal the initial premium received when the spread was established, $168.75. This is the maximum profit from this position. If the index closed below 230, all the options would expire worthless and your account would equal the premium received when the spread was initiated, $168.75. Exhibit 2-17 summarizes this technique.

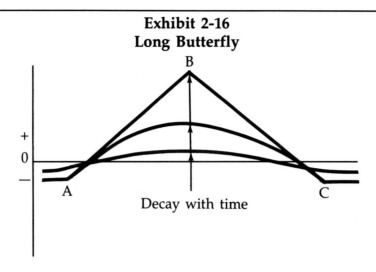

Exhibit 2-16
Long Butterfly

SITUATION: Anticipate little index movement.

OBJECTIVE: To gain premium income from decay of options.

STRATEGY: Sell two call options and simultaneously buy identical call options at the next highest and lowest strike prices.

ANALYSIS: The long butterfly profits from the decay of the middle strike options. The two options purchased protect the investment from significant loss if the index changes dramatically.

RISK/RETURN: If the index changes dramatically, the loss is limited to the initial cost of the spread. The maximum return is achieved when the index value equals the strike of the middle strike options at expiration.

EXAMPLE:
Buy one S&P 500 240 call at $0.6875 on October 5
Buy one S&P 500 230 call at $6.125 on October 5
Sell two S&P 500 235 calls at $2.5625 each on October 5

Index value remains at 235 when options expire.

Exercise 230 call for $5.00
All other options expire worthless

Profit = $5.00 × 100 = $500.00 − $168.75 (cost) = $331.25

Exhibit 2-17
Short Butterfly

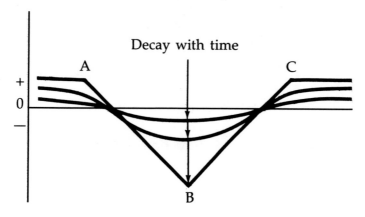

SITUATION: Anticipate significant index movement.

OBJECTIVE: To gain premium income from decay of options.

STRATEGY: Buy two call options and simultaneously sell identical call options at the next highest and lowest strike prices.

ANALYSIS: The short butterfly profits from the decay of the options sold. The two options purchased protect the investment from significant loss if the index doesn't change.

RISK/RETURN: If the index remains unchanged, the loss is limited to the initial income from the spread minus value of the out-of-the-money options. Maximum return is achieved when the index value is above that of the high strike option or below the low strike option.

EXAMPLE:
Sell one S&P 500 240 call at $0.6875 on October 5
Sell one S&P 500 230 call at $6.125 on October 5
Buy two S&P 500 235 calls at $2.5625 each on October 5

Index value moves from 235 to 245 when options expire.

Exercise 235 calls for $10.00 each.
Pay 240 option holder $5.00
Pay 230 option holder $15.00

Profit = $168.75 initial value of spread. All premiums cancel at expiration.

Choosing the correct speculative strategy for a given market opinion is not difficult once you are familiar with the techniques. Exhibit 2-18 summarizes the strategies and corresponding market opinions discussed in this chapter. The key to successful speculation is having discipline, following the principles discussed earlier, and, of course, having good instincts about future market movements.

Exhibit 2-18
Summary of Speculative Strategies

Strategy	Situation Anticipated
Buy Calls	Strong increase
Buy Puts	Strong decline
Sell Calls	Neutral or small decline
Sell Puts	Neutral or small increase
Buy Straddle	Major movement, direction uncertain
Sell Straddle	No movement
Buy Strangle	Major movement, direction uncertain
Sell Strangle	No movement
Vertical Call/Debit	Moderate increase
Vertical Call/Credit	Little movement or slight decline
Vertical Put/Debit	Moderate decline
Vertical Put/Credit	Moderate increase
Horizontal Call/Debit	Moderate increase
Horizontal Put/Debit	Moderate decline
Long Butterfly	No movement
Short Butterfly	Major movement

PROBLEMS & QUESTIONS

---

1. What should a speculator do before selecting a speculation strategy?
2. What is the primary risk in buying index options? selling index options? Does the passing of time help you or hurt you when you buy index options? sell them?
3. What is the difference between a straddle and a strangle? What impact does this difference have on the risk/return trade-off?
4. Locate the index option listing in *The Wall Street Journal*. Select an out-of-the-money call and put option from one of the listings. List the premium for each option and the corresponding index value in a notebook. After a few days check the premiums of those options. If you had purchased these options, what would your return be? What would the return be if you sold the options? What is the risk of each position?
5. Practice each of the remaining speculative strategies using the same data source. Which strategy was the most profitable? Which strategies lost money? Why? Repeat the process when the index value moves in the opposite direction. Which strategies provided the most profit or the most loss? Why? From this analysis, which strategies seem to have the most risk (variation in return)? the least risk?

Chapter
Three

HEDGING STRATEGIES

Stock index options are used by managers of stock portfolios (individual or institutional) to transfer unwanted price risk to market speculators. Portfolio managers transfer this undesirable price risk (protect the portfolio from adverse price changes) by *hedging*. Stock index options provide many practical and effective ways of hedging portfolios.

This chapter will acquaint you with how stock index options are used in portfolio hedging strategies. Emphasis is on how the risk/return position of the portfolio is altered by hedging and the specific market conditions suitable for each hedging technique. Using stock index options to enhance return and to assume market positions prior to receiving funds is discussed.

HEDGING PRINCIPLES

The speculator tries to profit from betting on market movements. The hedger attempts to protect his/her portfolio from adverse market movements. A market speculator will realize substantial profits if the market predictions are correct. A hedger already has a position in the market (the portfolio of stocks). His objective is protecting this investment from adverse price changes.

Suppose you own a portfolio of stocks. You will realize a profit if the value of your portfolio increases and suffer a loss if the value declines. If you could protect your portfolio from decreases in value without foregoing the opportunity to gain if the portfolio increases in value, you could increase your profit potential. Protecting your portfolio against the possibility of loss is the essence of hedging.

Hedging a portfolio of stocks is very similar to buying an insurance policy. If you have health insurance, you are protecting your income against the possibility of incurring substantial health care expenses. The risk is transferred to the insurance company. The cost associated with transferring this risk is the premium on your insurance policy. You are willing to forego some current income by paying the insurance premium in order to protect yourself from incurring potentially substantial health care costs. If you don't get sick, you would have lost some income (insurance premiums) but your risk was reduced.

If you hedge a portfolio of stocks, you forego some return to protect yourself against adverse price movement. You will preserve your portfolio if prices decline by transferring that risk to someone else (usually a market speculator). Thus, using stock index options in conjunction with a portfolio of stocks in a hedging program is a conservative approach to investing that focuses on reducing risk without reducing the opportunity for profit.

PORTFOLIO RISK

Our goal in a hedging program is to control risk of loss from adverse price movements. Any single stock involves risk from two general sources. First, **company-specific factors** are unique to the company issuing the security, for example, a strike or a major loss due to a natural disaster. On the other hand, something good may happen to that particular company, such as discovering oil on some land that they own. Company-specific risk is **unsystematic risk**.

Stocks may also be affected by **market** or **systematic risk**, which has an impact on all stocks to some degree. The general level of economic activity, energy prices, interest rates, and inflation are examples of market factors that affect all securities. The total risk of a stock is equal to its specific (unsystematic) risk plus market (systematic) risk, as shown in Exhibit 3-1.

Exhibit 3-1
Total Risk

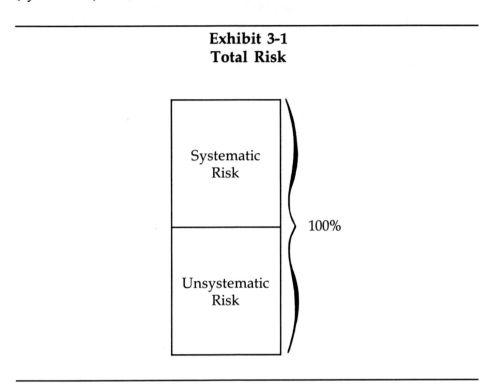

If an investor only owned one stock, it would be easy to determine his overall risk, which would be equal to the total risk (market plus specific) of the issuing company. However, most investors own portfolios of stocks. Their concern is the return on the *entire* portfolio.

How do we measure the risk of an entire portfolio? The key is to realize that the behavior of some stocks offsets the movement of others. At any point in time, some stocks increase, others decline, and some are unchanged. For example, suppose you own the portfolio of stocks listed in Exhibit 3-2.

If company A suffers a major loss due to a company-specific factor and its stock price declines to $10 per share, the value of the portfolio will decline to $9,000 (a 10 percent loss). However, if you had invested all of the original $10,000 in company A, you would have suffered a $5,000 (50 percent) loss. By diversifying you have reduced the impact a company-specific factor can have on overall portfolio return. As mentioned, company-specific risk is reduced when an investor owns a diversified portfolio of stocks. This is shown in Exhibit 3-3.

Exhibit 3-2

Stock	Price	Shares	Value
A	$20	100	· $2,000
B	21	100	2,100
C	18	100	1,800
D	41	100	4,100
Total Portfolio Value			$10,000

Exhibit 3-3
Portfolio Risk Versus Diversification

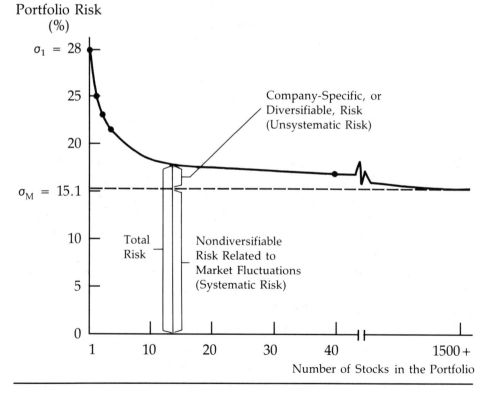

You can see in the exhibit only market risk remains in a well-diversified portfolio. Therefore, the relevant risk of an individual security is its sensitivity to market factors, or the degree to which it tends to move with the market.

Are all stocks equally risky in the sense that adding them to a portfolio would have an identical effect on the portfolio's riskiness? The answer is no, different stocks will have different effects on the portfolio's overall risk. What we are concerned with, then, is measuring the additional market risk a stock contributes to the portfolio.

The tendency of a stock to move with the market is measured by its beta coefficient, which reflects the stock's volatility or the degree to which it moves with the market. The beta coefficient for the market is equal to 1.0, by definition. If you owned all the stocks in the market, a 10 percent increase in your portfolio would obviously accompany a 10 percent increase in the market because the two would move together. With a beta of 1.0 as a benchmark, the risk an individual stock contributes to a portfolio can be measured by determining a stock's beta. If a stock has a beta greater than 1.0, it is considered riskier than an average stock. If a stock has a beta less than 1.0, it is considered less risky. Betas for some well-known firms are shown in Exhibit 3-4.

Exhibit 3-4
Company Betas

Company	Beta
Amoco Corporation	1.20
Exxon Corporation	0.80
Mobil Corporation	1.05
McDonald's	1.00
American Brands	0.70
Phillip Morris	0.90
American Broadcasting	1.15
CBS Inc.	1.05
Boeing Corporation	1.15
Lockheed	1.20

Source: *Value Line Investment Survey,* 1986

Betas for thousands of companies are calculated and published
by Value Line and the major brokerage firms. If you own stock in
some companies that do not have published betas, you can easily
calculate this value yourself. Plotting the return of a stock against
the return on the market (using the S & P 500 as a proxy) yields
a scatter diagram like the one shown in Exhibit 3-5.

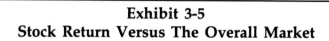

Exhibit 3-5
Stock Return Versus The Overall Market

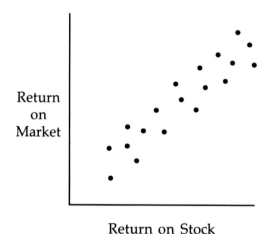

Return
on
Market

Return on Stock

Beta can be determined by measuring the slope of a line plotted
through these points. Many hand-held calculators can make this calculation. The specific procedure for doing this with either a Texas
Instruments or Hewlett-Packard calculator is described in Exhibit 3-6.

Exhibit 3-6
Determining Beta Using a Handheld Calculator

Texas Instruments

1. Press **2nd Mode** until "STAT" shows in the display.

2. Enter the first X value (index return), press x ⤸ y, and then enter the
   first Y value (stock return) and press Σ+.

3. Repeat Step 2 until all values have been entered.

4. Press **2nd b/a** to find the value of the Y intercept and then press x $ y to display the beta.

Hewlett-Packard 12C

1. Press **f Clx** to clear the memory.

2. Enter the first Y value (stock return), press **Enter,** and then enter the first X value (index return) and press Σ+.

3. Repeat step 2 until all values have been entered.

4. Press **O g ŷ,r** to find the Y intercept.

5. Press **STO 0** to store the Y intercept value.

6. Press **RCL 0 CHS x $ y** - to calculate and display the beta.

You can calculate the portfolio beta to determine the sensitivity of a portfolio to changes in the market. As shown in Exhibit 3-7, a portfolio beta is the weighted average of the betas for the individual stocks in the portfolio.

Exhibit 3-7
Determining Beta of Total Portfolio

Stock	Price	Value	Beta
A	$20	$2,000	1.20
B	21	2,100	0.90
C	18	1,800	1.15
D	41	4,100	1.00
Portfolio Beta			1.05

Index options can be a low-cost alternative for adjusting your portfolio beta. Suppose you own a portfolio that has a beta of 1.35. In a short-run market decline, your portfolio will suffer above-average losses. However, if you could reduce the beta of your portfolio during the market decline, your losses would be reduced. This can be done by combining index options with the securities in your portfolio, which transfers the risk of a market decline to a speculator.

To use stock index options to adjust your portfolio beta, you must find an optionable index that closely coincides with your portfolio. Identifying the best index for the hedging program requires determining one more characteristic of your portfolio.

CORRELATION

A hedging program involves assuming positions in stock index options that will be profitable under certain market conditions which will lead to losses in your portfolio. With the hedged position profits from index options offset the portfolio losses if the expected market conditions occur. If market conditions differ from what you expect, the hedged position will probably be less profitable than an unhedged position. This is a cost of transferring risk to speculators.

For any hedging program to be successful, the hedging instrument, in this case, index options, must move like your portfolio. If you predict a market decline and want to hedge against this, then you must select an index that is similar to your portfolio. If a 10 percent market decline leads to a 10 percent decline in the value of your portfolio, you would like a position in index options that gives a 10 percent profit when the market declines. This is a perfect hedge. If a 10 percent market decline resulted in a 5 percent profit in the index options position, you would still sustain some loss (5 percent). To avoid this, you must select the hedging index that has the highest degree of association or **correlation** with your portfolio. You can do this by determining the **correlation coefficient** of your portfolio with several optionable indexes.

The correlation coefficient is a statistical term for the degree to which two variables coincide. Values for the coefficient range from -1 to $+1$. If two variables have a correlation coefficient of $+1$, then they are perfectly positively correlated. This means that when one variable changes, the other changes in exactly the same way. If two variables have a correlation coefficient of −1, they are perfectly negatively correlated, which means they move in exactly opposite directions.

Exhibit 3-8 shows this graphically. Part A is a scatter diagram showing a perfectly positively correlated relationship of returns over time. Part B shows a perfectly negatively correlated relationship. Since perfect correlation, positive or negative, is rare in the stock market these extremes are useful only to illustrate the concept.

Exhibit 3-8
Perfect Positive (A) and Negative (B) Correlation

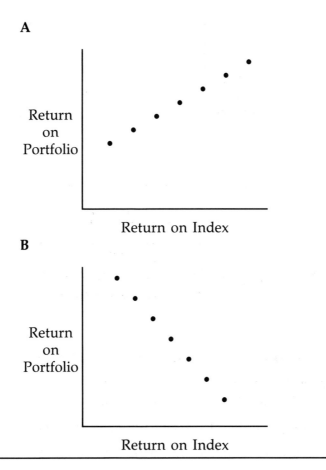

Since correlation of most stocks is less than perfect, a plot would be more likely to resemble the scatter diagram shown in Exhibit 3-9. As stated earlier, to select the appropriate index for a hedging program, you must determine the correlation coefficient between your portfolio and various indexes. The procedure for doing this using a Texas Instruments or Hewlett-Packard calculator is shown in Exhibit 3-10.

Exhibit 3-9
Typical Correlation Between a Stock and The Overall Market

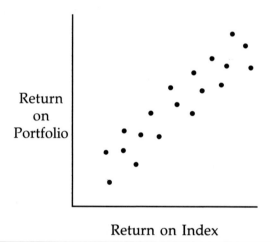

Return on Index

Exhibit 3-10
**Determining the Correlation Coefficient of an Index
and the Overall Portfolio**

Texas Instruments

1. Press **2nd Mode** until "STAT" shows on the display.

2. Enter the first X value (index return), press x ⥮ y, and then enter the first Y value (stock return) and press Σ+.

3. Repeat Step 2 until all values have been entered.

4. Press **2nd Corr** to obtain the correlation coefficient.

Hewlett-Packard 12C

1. Press **f Clx** to clear the memory.

2. Enter the first Y value (stock return), press **Enter,** and then enter the first X value (index return) and press Σ+.

3. Repeat step 2 until all values have been entered.

4. Press **O g ŷ,r** to find the Y intercept.

5. Press **STO 0** to store the Y intercept value.

6. Press **O g ŷ,r** - to obtain the correlation coefficient.

Suppose your portfolio yields the monthly rates of return listed in Exhibit 3-11. You are interested in the S & P 100 which is highly correlated with your portfolio and thus, a good index to use in a hedging program. Using the information in Exhibit 3-11 and the procedures for calculating the correlation coefficient described in Exhibit 3-10, determine the correlation coefficient.

Exhibit 3-11
Rates of Return
for Example Portfolio and S&P 100 Index

Month	Portfolio A	S&P 100
June	.30%	.40%
July	1.82	1.43
August	.91	1.90
September	− .06	−1.47
October	−1.53	−2.65
November	3.31	3.72
December	.61	2.38
January	.32	− .72
February	1.48	.66
March	2.41	2.05
April	1.80	3.06
Mean	.98%	.98%
Standard Deviation	1.38%	1.96%

You should have found a correlation coefficient value equal to .904. This indicates that the S & P 100 is highly correlated with your portfolio. As mentioned, the index that best correlates with your portfolio should be used in a hedging program. Therefore, other indexes should be tested before you make a choice.

Given this information on selecting options, we can turn to a discussion of specific hedging strategies.

HEDGING STRATEGIES

Most investors want to transfer the risk of a market decline. Since we are concerned about losing portfolio value in this case, hedging this risk involves establishing a position in stock index options that will achieve profits when the market declines. The two most common strategies for accomplishing this are covered call writing and protective put purchasing.

COVERED CALL WRITING When you write stock index call options, you receive the premium on the option. If the option expires out of the money, the entire premium is income for your account. Index call options expire out of the money when the strike price is higher than the current value of the index. Therefore, if you expect the value of an index to stay the same or decline, you should write calls to gain premium income. This index income should largely offset portfolio losses if the two are highly correlated. To illustrate, suppose you own the portfolio listed in Exhibit 3-12. The current market value of this 15-stock portfolio is $50,000, it has a beta of approximately 1.0, and it has a correlation coefficient of .91 with the S & P 100 stock index. If you anticipate a stable market or a small market decline and want to enhance the return on your portfolio, S & P 100 index options can be used.

Exhibit 3-12
Sample Portfolio for Covered Call Writing

Stock	Price	Shares	Value
A	$20	200	$ 4,000
B	21	100	2,100

C	18	100	1,800
D	41	100	4,100
E	75	200	15,000
F	8	500	4,000
G	17	300	5,100
H	32	100	3,200
I	38	100	3,800
J	69	100	6,900
Portfolio Value			$50,000

The current value of the S & P 100 index is 220 and the premium on a 220 call option with one month to expiration is 1.50. By writing two S & P 100 call options you would gain $300 in premium value. Two options are written since the value of each option contract is $22,000 (220 times $100) so that the total value of the two contracts is close to the value of your portfolio. If the call option expired when the index value was 220, the entire $300 would be yours (less commission). The $300 premium gained from the sale of the calls would enhance the return on your portfolio. This is described in greater detail in Exhibit 3-13.

Exhibit 3-13
Covered Call Writing

SITUATION: Anticipate slight market decline.

OBJECTIVE: To protect portfolio value in a declining market.

STRATEGY: Sell call options on an index highly correlated with your portfolio.

ANALYSIS: Select index to use in the hedge. The number of calls sold is determined by the total contract value which should approximate the value of your portfolio.

RISK/RETURN: If the market declines as anticipated, the loss on your portfolio will be offset by the premium income received from the call option. If the market rises, your profit potential is limited by the call option.

EXAMPLE:

Current Value of Portfolio: $50,000
Portfolio Beta: 1.0

Anticipate market decline.

Sell two OEX 220 calls for $1.50   Index Value = 220
Contract Value: $44,000

At expiration the index value equals 218 (1% decline).
You gain $300 premium income.

Portfolio value at expiration equals $49,500 ($500 loss).

Net Portfolio Value = $49,500 + $300 = $49,800.

If the market (index) value increased after this position was established, the option position would reduce some of the profit from your portfolio. Suppose that the market increased 5 percent by the time your options expired. The index value would be 5 percent higher than 220, or 231. You would owe the option holder $1,100 per option or $2,200 in total. Your loss on the options position would equal $2,200 minus the initial $300 received or $1,900. However, in most cases, the value of your portfolio would have increased. If it also increased by 5 percent, it would be worth $52,500. The $2,500 increase in your portfolio value would offset the $1,900 loss on the options for a total profit of $600 for the month. This transaction is summarized in Exhibit 3-14.

Exhibit 3-14
Covered call writing (5% market increase)

Current Value of Portfolio: $50,000
Portfolio Beta: 1.0

Anticipate market decline.

Sell two OEX 220 calls for $1.50   Index Value = 220
Contract Value: $44,000

At expiration the index value equals 231 (5% increase).
Option Value = $1,100 (231 − 220 × $100) per option.

Portfolio value at expiration equals $52,500 (5% increase).

Net Portfolio Value = $52,500 − $2,200 = $50,300.

If the market had declined by 5 percent over the month, the option would expire worthless and you would receive the $300 premium as income. Your portfolio probably would have declined in value as well, but the index income would partially offset that loss. Suppose the value of your portfolio declined by 5 percent, or $2,500. The $300 option income would reduce this loss to $2,200. Exhibit 3-15 summarizes this situation.

Exhibit 3-15
Covered call writing (5% market decline)

Current Value of Portfolio: $50,000
Portfolio Beta: 1.0

Anticipate market decline.

Sell two OEX 220 calls for $1.50   Index Value = 220
Contract Value: $44,000

At expiration the index value equals 209 (5% decline).
Option Value = $0.00

Portfolio value at expiration equals $47,500 (5% decline).

Net Portfolio Value = $47,500 − $300 = $47,800.

From these three scenarios it is obvious that covered call writing is a useful strategy for enhancing portfolio income when the market is expected to remain stable or decline slightly. The cost of this income is the lost opportunity for large gains when the market increases dramatically. Also, when the market falls dramatically, protection is limited.

Another risk concerns the correlation of the index and your portfolio. If the two are not highly correlated, there is a chance that the value of your portfolio will decline but the index value will increase, resulting in a loss on both the portfolio and the options. Therefore, the key to successfully applying this technique is locating a highly correlated optionable index.

PROTECTIVE PUT PURCHASES Buying put options is like buying insurance against sizable market declines. Hedging a portfolio against a market decline with put options insures the "floor" value of the portfolio without limiting the potential increase in portfolio value if the market should rise.

Suppose once again that you own the portfolio described in Exhibit 3-12. Remember that the portfolio has a beta of 1.0 and a .91 correlation coefficient with the S & P 100 index. The index value is equal to 220 and the premium on a 220 put with one month to expiration is $2.25.

To determine the number of options you should purchase, divide your portfolio value ($50,000) by the contract value of the put options, (220 × $100 = $22,000), and multiply that amount by the beta of the portfolio (1.0). This procedure is shown in Exhibit 3-16 for several different portfolios.

Exhibit 3-16
Determining Number of Protective Put Contracts to Buy

Portfolio Value	Portfolio Beta	Contract Value	Number of Puts
$ 50,000	1.0	$22,000	2
200,000	1.2	22,000	11
20,000	0.8	22,000	1
125,000	1.1	22,000	6

Based on the information in Exhibit 3-12, you should buy 2.27 contracts. Since partial options cannot be purchased, you will only buy two. This leaves a portion of the portfolio "uninsured," but the additional cost of another option is excessive.

Buying two options for 2.25 each reduces the value of your portfolio by $450. What have you purchased? Protection from market declines without sacrificing the opportunity for gain. Suppose the market declines by 5 percent. The value of the index should decline to 209. The value of your portfolio will also decline approximately 5 percent to $47,050 (remember the $450 premium charge). Both options would expire with a value of $11 each or $2,200 total. This profit would accrue to you and bring the value of your portfolio to $49,250. A portion of the portfolio was unhedged because partial options cannot be purchased, so the hedge is not perfect. Exhibit 3-17 illustrates this transaction.

Exhibit 3-17
Protective Puts (5% market decline)

Current Value of Portfolio: $50,000
Portfolio Beta: 1.0

Anticipate market decline.

Sell two OEX 220 calls for $2.25   Index Value = 220
Contract Value: $44,000

At expiration the index value equals 209 (5% increase).
Option Value = $1,100 per option.

Portfolio value at expiration equals $47,050 (5% decline – $450).

Net Portfolio Value = $47,050 + $2,200 = $49,250.

If the market declined by 10 percent, the value of your portfolio would have decreased to approximately $44,550. The index value would have declined to approximately 198. For each option held, you would gain the difference between the current index value, 198, and the strike price, 220, times $100. A 10 percent market decline leads to a $4,400 profit on the puts. This profit would bring the value of the portfolio back to $48,950. Therefore, purchasing put options provides protection against severe market declines. And you don't have to be able to predict the magnitude of the expected decline.

What if the market didn't decline, but rose 5 percent? The index would be 231 at expiration, so the put options would expire worthless. The $450 premium would be lost. However, the value of your portfolio would, on average, increase by 5 percent to $52,050, net of premium. The hedge cost you $450 of potential gain, but the portfolio still shared in the market rally.

If the market gained 10 percent, your portfolio would be worth approximately $54,550, net of premium. The most that the hedge can cost is $450. This premium protects the portfolio from dramatic market declines, but allows it to participate in market gains. These transactions are summarized in Exhibit 3-18.

Exhibit 3-18
Protective Puts (5 and 10 percent market increase)

Current Value of Portfolio: $50,000
Portfolio Beta: 1.0

Anticipate market decline.

Sell two OEX 220 calls for $2.25   Index Value = 220
Contract Value: $44,000

At expiration the index value equals 231 (5% increase).
Option Value = 0.00

Portfolio value at expiration equals $52,050 (5% increase − $450).

Net Portfolio Value = $52,050.

Current Value of Portfolio: $50,000
Portfolio Beta: 1.0

Anticipate market decline.

Sell two OEX 220 calls for $2.25   Index Value = 220
Contract Value: $44,000

At expiration the index value equals 242 (10% increase).
Option Value = $0.00

Portfolio value at expiration equals $54,550 (10% increase − $450).

Net Portfolio Value = $54,550.

One disadvantage of buying put options is that the hedge only has a value if market movement is significant. If the portfolio and the index stayed around 220 for any length of time, the amount paid would exceed the return from the portfolio, so that portfolio value would slowly decay. Also as mentioned, the index must be highly correlated with the portfolio. If it isn't, the portfolio value could decline and the index value could rise, leading to a loss on both positions.

Index put options can also be used to hedge a segment of your portfolio. Suppose you own the portfolio listed in Exhibit 3-19.

Notice that the portfolio is heavily weighted with energy stocks, that half of your investment, $25,000, is in energy stocks with an average beta of 1.25 and the rest is in other stocks with an average beta of 1.0.

Exhibit 3-19
Hedging a Segment of a Portfolio

Stock	Price	Shares	Value
A (Energy)	$20	150	$ 3,000
B	21	100	2,100
C	18	100	1,800
D	41	100	4,100
E (Energy)	75	200	15,000
F	10	500	5,000
G	17	300	5,100
H (Energy)	32	100	3,200
I (Energy)	38	100	3,800
J	69	100	6,900
Portfolio Value			$50,000
Energy Segment			25,000

If you expected energy stocks to suffer in the near term, you could purchase AMEX Oil & Gas index puts to protect that segment. If the AMEX Oil index value was 145 and puts with one month to expiration were selling for 1.5, you could purchase two put options for $300 and protect the value of the energy segment. The calculation for determining the number of options to be purchased is shown in Exhibit 3-20.

Exhibit 3-20
Protective Puts
(Determining Number of Contracts to Buy)

1. Energy Segment Value = $25,000

2. Contract Value = 145 × $100 = $14,500

3. Divide Segment Value by Contract Value = 25,000/14,500 = 1.72

4. Multiply by Segment Beta = 1.72 × 1.25 = 2.15 or 2 contracts.

EXAMPLES:

Segment Value	Segment Beta	Contract Value	Number of Puts
$ 50,000	1.0	$22,000	2
200,000	1.2	22,000	11
20,000	0.8	22,000	1
125,000	1.1	22,000	6

If the market remained stable, but the energy stocks suffered an average loss of 5 percent, you would be protected. Half of your portfolio would be unaffected, on average. The energy segment, worth $25,000, would decline in value to approximately $23,450, net of the $300 premium. The oil & gas index value would have fallen to 137.75. At expiration your put options would be worth 7.25 each, or $1,450 total. This profit would restore the value of your energy segment to $24,900. If energy stocks should rally, you will have forgone $300 profit to protect this segment. Some sample transactions for this technique are shown in Exhibit 3-21.

Exhibit 3-21
Segment Protection Using Puts

Current Value of Portfolio: $25,000
Portfolio Beta: 1.25

Anticipate market decline.

Buy two Oil & Gas 145 puts for $1.50   Index Value = 145
Contract Value: $14,500

At expiration the index value equals 137.75 (5% decline).
Option Value = $725 per option.

Segment value at expiration equals $23,450 (5% decline − $300).

Net Segment Value = $23,450 + $1,500 = $24,950.$450).

SUMMARY

Choosing the correct hedging strategy requires careful assessment of your portfolio in relation to market indexes. Given these characteristics, your opinion as to the nature of the current market situation will determine which hedge is appropriate.

Generally, if modest market declines are forecast, covered call writing is the most beneficial strategy. If dramatic declines are expected, protective puts are better.

PROBLEMS & QUESTIONS

---

1. What is the purpose of a hedging program?
2. How does the risk of a single stock differ from the risk of a portfolio of stocks? What impact does this difference have on a hedging program?
3. What is beta? Why is it important?
4. What is correlation? Why is it important?
5. List the current holdings in your portfolio (or a hypothetical portfolio). What is the portfolio beta? Does the composition of the portfolio appear to match one of the leading optionable indexes? How could you confirm this apparent match?
6. Given the index selected in Question 5, practice (on paper) a covered call hedge. Check the value of your portfolio and the option premiums one week later. Assuming the transaction is executed, what would be the result of the hedge?
7. Repeat the process above for a protective put purchase.

Chapter Four

MECHANICS

Detailed information on the mechanics of stock index option trading is needed before any option strategy can be implemented. These "nuts and bolts" must be discussed so the reader understands the additional risks and conventions of trading index options. This chapter provides a link between strategies discussed in the previous chapters and actual implementation.

OPENING AN INDEX OPTIONS ACCOUNT

Account representatives at most major brokerage houses are licensed to trade index options. Many discount brokers are also licensed to trade index options, while they will simply execute your order with minimal advice, commissions will generally be much smaller. Almost all brokerage houses require that customers meet some minimum financial standards when trading index options. This protects the customer and the firm from a major loss if the client is under-capitalized.

Opening a stock index option account involves signing a **standard option agreement**. Before you sign this document, you must acknowledge that you understand the risks of trading listed options and should not purchase or sell options unless you are able to sustain a total loss. This agreement informs you of the high risk in trading options and protects the brokerage house. If you want to open a hedging account, the brokerage house may impose additional requirements. A sample option agreement is shown in Exhibit 4-1. Most agreements follow this format, although some differences do exist.

Exhibit 4-1
Standard Option Agreement
Individual and Joint Accounts Only

Gentlemen:

In connection with any transaction executed by you on my behalf for the purchase and sales of put and call options. I agree as follows:

1. All transactions shall be subject to the constitution, rules, regulations, customs, and usages of the exchange, or market and its clearing house, if any, where executed. I further agree that I will not, either alone or in concert with others violate the position or exercise limits which the Exchange or marketplace where executed, may establish from time to time as set forth in the booklet "Understanding the Risks and Uses of Listed Options."

2. In the case of options sold or written by me in a cash account:

    (a) With respect to a call option which if exercised against me will require the delivery of securities sold. I will keep such securities in my account with you until the expiration of the option period, and will not sell or withdraw such securities. If the option is exercised, you may deliver such securities to the purchaser without previous notice to me.

    (b) With respect to any put option which if exercised against me will require payment for securities purchased. I will keep in my account sufficient funds for such payment until the expiration of the option period, and will not withdraw such funds or utilize them for any purpose. If the option is exercised you may use such funds for the purchase of such securities without previous notice to me.

3. Any securities and funds held by you in any account of mine with you shall be held by you as security for the performance by me of my obligations to you under this agreement.

4. As option transactions involve a high degree of risk, I understand that:

    (a) I should not purchase an option unless I am able to sustain a total loss of the premium and transaction costs, and I should not write a call option unless I either own the underlying security (or a security convertible, exchangeable, or exercisable into such underlying security) or am able to sustain substantial financial losses, and that I should not write a put option unless I am able to sustain substantial financial losses.

    (b) I may not be able to close a position in the event that a secondary market in the option ceases to exist or the listing exchange restricts or suspends trading in the option.

5. I have been advised of and agree to abide by your policies and federal regulations regarding margining of options and related transactions.

6. I agree to advise you of any changes in my financial situation and needs, experience, or investment objectives.

7. In case of my insolvency, death or attachment of my property, you may, with respect to any pending options, take such steps as you consider necessary to protect yourself against loss.

8. Any agreement by me with you, whether previously or hereafter made applicable to any account of mine with you, shall also apply to such option transactions except to the extent which it conflicts with this agreement. In the event of a conflict, this agreement shall control, and where this is no conflict, each provision of each agreement shall apply.

9. Except to the extent that controversies involving claims arising under the Federal Securities Laws may be litigated, any controversy between us arising out of such option transactions or this agreement shall be settled by arbitration only before the National Association of Securities Dealers, Incorporated, or the New York Stock Exchange, or an Exchange located in the United States upon which listed options transactions are executed. We shall have the right of election as to which of the foregoing tribunals shall conduct the arbitration. Such election is to be by registered mail, addressed to Merrill Lynch's head office at 165 Broadway, New York, N.Y. 10080, attention of the Law Department. The notice of election is to be postmarked five days after the date of your demand to make such election. At the expiration of the five days, we hereby authorize Merrill Lynch to make such election on our behalf.

10. I understand that exercise assignment notices for options contracts are allocated among customer short positions in accordance with the date of the transaction which established the short position. Positions which were established earliest will be assigned first ("First-In, First-Out"). A more detailed description of MLPF&S's allocation procedure is available upon request.

11. Absent the written designation of an agent to transact business on my behalf (power of attorney), I alone may make trading decisions in my account; however, unless I give specific instructions to the contrary, you may exercise discretion in the selection of the exchange or marketplace for the execution of dually traded options.

12. This agreement and its enforcement shall be governed by the laws of the State of New York.

13. With regard to the exercise of index option contracts, I understand that I must advise you no later than 3:45 P.M. New York time of my intent to exercise 25 or more contracts in the same series on that day. I understand that exercises in all accounts subject to my control will be aggregated in determining whether 25 or more contracts are involved.

I (WE) HAVE RECEIVED AND READ THE BOOKLET "UNDERSTANDING THE RISKS AND USES OF LISTED OPTIONS" AND ARE AWARE OF THE SPECIAL RISKS ATTENDANT TO OPTION TRADING. THE STATEMENTS CONTAINED ON THIS FORM ARE ACCURATE.

CUSTOMER'S SIGNATURE	DATE SIGNED	SPOUSE'S SIGNATURE (REQUIRED FOR JOINT ACCOUNTS)	DATE SIGNED

Once you sign the option agreement and it is approved by the brokerage house, you may trade index options. Exhibit 4-2 shows how an option transaction is executed. The process is remarkably efficient. After you give an order to your broker, he or she transmits it to the exchange trading that particular index option. When the order reaches the exchange, the floor broker in the pit is notified and attempts to fill it by open outcry. If another trader in the option pit is willing to take the order, a transaction is completed. Your broker is notified and confirms the order to you over the phone. Written confirmation is forwarded within a few days. The entire process of entering an order to receiving oral confirmation usually takes less than 10 minutes if the order is filled immediately.

Exhibit 4-2
Executing a Stock Index Option Transaction

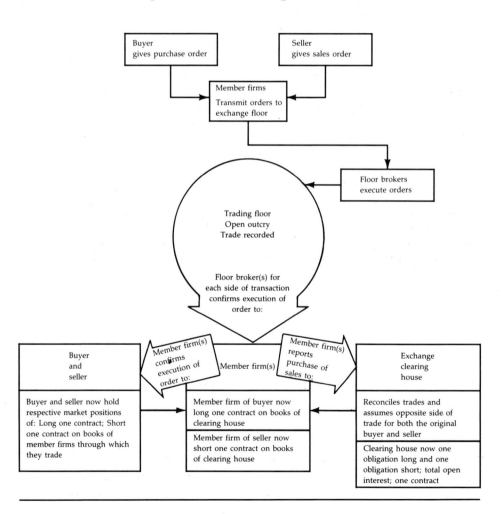

Transactions do not take place directly between floor brokers. Instead, a clearing agency, regulated by the Securities and Exchange Commission, issues all standardized options. This Options Clearing Corporation (OCC) is technically the buyer and seller of all listed options. The OCC provides both buyers and sellers with assurance that option contracts will be honored. If the credibility of every individual investor were at stake, then the market would in all likelihood be very small and inefficient.

The obligations of option writers are guaranteed by a group of brokerage houses called ''clearing members.'' To be a clearing member, a firm must meet several financial tests and deposit margins or other collateral with the OCC to back up option writers' positions. In addition, each firm must contribute to a special fund that provides capital to the OCC in the event that a clearing member fails. This fund and margin collateral are the OCC reserve against nonperformance on an option contract.

Since brokerage houses are liable directly to the OCC in the event of a nonperformance, they screen clients carefully. This is why all brokerage firms require a standard option agreement which protects the firm if a client fails to perform on an option contract.

TYPES OF ORDERS   You can place several different types of orders with a broker. Some of these specialized orders will reduce the risk of strategies discussed earlier. The most common types of orders are listed below.

Market—Order to buy or sell at the prevailing market price; used in highly liquid markets. Caution must be exercised if the option is not traded frequently. Floor traders may take advantage of market orders on inactive options for which reported prices may not reflect actual transaction prices because the options are not liquid.

Limit—Order to buy or sell at a specific price or better.

Stop—Order to buy or sell once a specific market price is reached; commonly used to prevent excessive losses or automatically initiate new positions.

Day—Order is good for one day only; that is, if the order is not filled by the close of trading that day, it is canceled.

These four basic types of orders, illustrated in Exhibit 4-3, should satisfy most of your needs in any speculative or hedging program. However, there are several more specific types of orders that you may find useful as your trading experience grows.

Exhibit 4-3
Sample Stock Index Option Orders

1. Buy one December S&P 500 220 call at market.
2. Buy one February Major Market Index 320 put at 4.
3. Sell one December S&P 500 220 call at 230 stop.
4. Buy one January S&P 500 220 straddle at market.

FEATURES OF STOCK INDEX OPTION CONTRACTS

Numerous specifications differentiate each index option contract. However, as we will see, option contracts also have many elements in common.

MARGIN REQUIREMENTS   Buyers of put and call index options must deposit 100 percent of the option premium. Unlike stock options, index options cannot be covered due to the nature of the underlying index. Thus, covered call writing is not used. Instead, most brokerage firms require 100 percent of the current premium plus 10 percent of the current contract value. The latter percentage may be reduced if the option is out of the money. Positions are marked to the market daily to reflect current option premium and index levels. Option writers are subject to margin calls if positions move unfavorably.

As an example, suppose you write the call option straddle described in Exhibit 4-4. Remember, with this strategy you are predicting that the index value will be at or near the strike price of the straddle at expiration. The total margin required (we are assuming 10 percent of contract value) is equal to the two option premiums, $1,300, plus 10 percent of the combined contract value, $4,400 (.10 × $44,000), for a total margin of $5,700. Your account is credited with the amount of the premium received from the option buyer, $1,300, so the net initial margin requirement is $4,400.

Exhibit 4-4
Margin Requirements—Index Option Straddle

Sell one 220 call at 6.75 $ 675.00
Sell one 220 put at 6.25   625.00
Total premium $1,300.00
Current index value = 220.
Index multiplier = 100
Total contract value = 220 × 100 = $22,000 each.
Required margin = 10% of $22,000 = $2,200 × 2 options = $5,700.
Total required margin = $4,400 plus $1,300 premium = $5,700.

Suppose that the index value changes dramatically the next day. The new option premiums and index level are listed in Exhibit 4-5. Since the index value has increased to 230 and the combined value of the premiums has increased to $1,600, your account has a deficit margin of $500. If your broker requires maintaining the original margin, you would have to deposit an additional $500 into your account or the broker would be forced to close out your position. If you are unavailable when the broker calls you for additional margin, your position may be closed out without your knowledge.

Exhibit 4-5
Margin Requirements—Index Option Straddle One Day Later

220 call at 14.75 $1,475.00
220 put at 1.25   125.00
Total premium $1,600.00
Current index value = 230.
Index multiplier = 100
Total contract value = 220 × 100 = $23,000 each.
Required margin = 10% of $23,000 = $2,300 × 2 options = $4,600.
Total required margin = $4,600 plus $1,600 premium = $6,200.

EXERCISE AND SETTLEMENT With respect to settlement, the major difference between stock options and stock index options is that index contracts are settled in cash. In contrast, stock options require delivery of the underlying stock. When a buyer exercises an index option, he or she is entitled to the in-the-money difference between the exercise price and the current index value at the close of trading on the day of exercise, times 100. Suppose you exercise an S&P 500 call with a strike of 220. At the close of trading that day, the index value is equal to 230. You would receive $100 times 100 or $1,000.

Actual settlement of index options takes place one business day after the option is exercised, under the auspices of OCC. The one-day lag and cash settlement create an additional risk for option writers, so-called **settlement risk.** The option buyer is entitled to the difference between the exercise price and the index value on the day of expiration. If the index value declines before the option writer is notified of the exercise, the writer is still liable for the value of the index **on the exercise date.** This timing risk limits option writers' ability to protect themselves when options are settled on a cash basis. This risk makes it more difficult to apply some of the speculative strategies that require short positions in index options.

TAX CONSIDERATIONS   The tax consequences of a stock index option transaction depend upon several factors. The extent of tax liability depends on whether the option is sold, exercised, or allowed to expire and whether the transaction qualifies as a hedging technique. Some exchanges provide information on the tax treatment of index options under various conditions. These pamphlets may be obtained directly from the exchange or from your broker. Since the tax consequences of any option transaction directly affect returns, you should consult with your broker or a tax expert *before* you adopt an index option strategy.

SPECIAL RISKS OF STOCK INDEX OPTIONS

In addition to the timing risk discussed previously, trading index options entails other risks that are unrelated to price movements. The most important of these are discussed below.

TRADING HALTS   Exchanges may halt trading on index options when the current value of the index is unavailable or when trading in a particular stock included in an index exceeds a specified percentage of the total index value. Trading may also be stopped if the exchange determines that fair and orderly market activity has been disrupted.

If trading is halted, the holders and writers of index options cannot close out their positions. Since trading in the stocks that make up an index may continue during this halt, index investors can incur substantial losses if the value of the underlying index moves adversely before trading resumes.

Option holders can exercise their options on the day before expiration, even if trading is still interrupted. However, if the trading halt is related to suspended trading on one or more of the stocks that make up the index and that trading has not resumed, the index value is calculated using the last available price for that stock. As a result, a portion of the index value will be based on current prices and another on noncurrent information.

LIQUIDITY   Daily trading in some stock index options is very low. This lack of liquidity may cause a number of problems. Option premiums are reported using the most recent transaction as a benchmark. If this transaction is not current because volume is low, the actual premium available in the option pit may be different from the reported premiums. Even with high-volume index options, certain strike prices or maturities may not be actively traded. As a general rule, the maturity with the fewest trading days remaining and the strike prices closest to the current index value account for most trading volume.

Another problem with low liquidity relates to the types of orders individual investors normally make. Most of the time, you will enter a market order with your transaction instructions. If the particular option you wish to trade has low liquidity and you enter a market order, the floor traders may profit at your expense by offering a price a bit higher or lower than should be offered in a market with higher volume (i.e., more traders). Your broker should be able to assist you in determining the appropriate order for the particular option you wish to trade.

ADJUSTMENTS   Stocks may be added to or deleted from an index. Most of the time these adjustments will not materially affect the stability of the index. However, the OCC may determine that an adjustment has materially affected the stability of an index and halt trading. The OCC may also alter the rights and obligations of option writers and holders if it feels the adjustment has significantly affected the index. This could result in abnormal losses to option writers and holders if the OCC action adversely affects the terms of their option contract.

OPENING PROCEDURES   On any given day, Exchanges can open trading on stock index options before trading on the stocks that make up the index has begun. In such cases, the reported value of the index is determined using the most recent price for those stocks that have not yet started trading on that day. The index will consequently be based on noncurrent price information and its value may change substantially once trading on the underlying stocks opens. Trading on index information that is not current increases the risk of assuming positions in stock index options.

BROKER INSOLVENCY   If your broker or the clearing member of the OCC that carries your broker's account becomes insolvent, some or all of your index option positions may be closed out without your consent. Even if your position is not closed out, you could experience significant delays or other problems in attempting to exercise options or close out your position. This reemphasizes the importance of selecting a brokerage house on the basis of more than low commissions. The cost of insolvency could be quite dramatic if your positions are closed out when index values are unfavorable.

MAINTAINING INFORMATION

Numerous sources of information on stock index options, ranging from price reporting to advisory newsletters, are available. The information you need depends on the strategy you are using and the size of your investment. Daily price quotations are available from many sources at a nominal cost. If you need more frequent updates, some services can provide quotes of transactions that occurred within the last few minutes. Obviously, more frequent updates are more expensive.

Advisory services may offer market predictions and strategy suggestions on a weekly basis. Others provide the same service over the telephone with continuous updating. Once again, the cost of these services varies with the frequency of the updates.

PROBLEMS & QUESTIONS

---

1. Why is the Options Clearing Corporation important?
2. What types of orders can be placed?
3. Suppose you want to initiate a short straddle strategy.
   Using data from *The Wall Street Journal* for one of the indexes, what would be your required margin? How does the required margin change?
4. What is settlement risk and why is it important?
5. What risks not related to price are important for index option traders?

Chapter
Five

CASE STUDIES

The four previous chapters have provided a comprehensive summary of how stock index options may be incorporated into individual portfolio management. To further help you recognize situations where index options may be used, two case studies are presented, which involve typical speculative and hedging applications. These case studies involve Brian Chadwick and Steve Tyson, who were introduced in the Prologue. Although their situations are briefly recapped here, you are urged to reread the Prologue before proceeding with the case studies.

BRIAN CHADWICK

Brian Chadwick, 35, has been investing in the stock market for several years. He has always invested conservatively in blue-chip companies with stable histories. Brian's portfolio is outlined in Exhibit 5-1. At this point in his career he has achieved financial security and has several years of experience investing in equities. He would now like to take advantage of this situation by "playing the market" a bit. However, Brian does not want to commit a large sum of money, at least until he determines whether his new investing strategy warrants taking on more risk. He decides that he is satisfied with his current stock holdings; thus, any funds for speculative investments must be restricted to the $3,000 in his money market fund. However, he doesn't feel comfortable risking all $3,000, and decides that $2,000 is the maximum he is willing to risk.

Exhibit 5-1

Stock	Value
IBM	$ 3,750
Exxon	1,200
General Motors	2,790
Minnesota Mining	3,260
USX	1,800
Alcoa	2,100
General Electric	1,680
Proctor & Gamble	2,440
Phillip Morris	1,100
Goodyear	2,220
Total value	$22,340

Now that he has identified the amount of money available for speculation, he begins investigating the different alternatives available to him. Over the course of a few weeks, Brian talks with several friends and associates about potential speculative vehicles. From these discussions he compiles a list of feasible alternatives, shown in Exhibit 5-2.

Exhibit 5-2
Speculative Investment Alternatives

Commodity Futures
Penny Stocks
Real Estate:
    Undeveloped Land
    Office Buildings
Precious Metals
Art
Stock Options
Stock Index Futures
Stock Index Options

Brian feels that he can quickly eliminate several of these alternatives. Investing in commodity futures was mentioned by several friends as a popular speculative vehicle. However, Brian does not feel comfortable with a vehicle that tracks commodities since he doesn't follow this market regularly and just plain doesn't understand the intricacies of commodity pricing. So this alternative is out.

Investing in penny stocks was also a popular alternative among his friends with speculative investments. Once again, this doesn't seem to be a good idea for Brian. He doesn't follow the penny stock market regularly and doesn't know how to select companies in this market. Investing in a company he knows little about in a market he doesn't follow is to Brian a pure gamble. He can't take advantage of any of the skills he has developed over his years of investing in blue-chip stocks.

Brian wants to limit his alternatives to take advantage of his experience in stock investing. This rules out all of the alternatives except for stock options, index futures, and index options. Brian has invested in stock options before. His experience was limited to using covered call writing to enhance his portfolio income. Brian felt comfortable with this portfolio hedging strategy. His previous experience with stock options provided a good foundation for applying this vehicle in speculative situations.

For Brian, there was a problem with incorporating stock options in a speculative trading program because there are too many alternative investments. How should he decide which companies to include in his speculative portfolio? Where would he obtain up-to-date and detailed information on the specific characteristics of each company? After he selects the companies, how will he determine when to replace a company in his portfolio? The amount of time needed to prepare and update the portfolio intimidated Brian.

The problems associated with stock options forced Brian to focus more on the nature of his speculating program. What did he want to "bet" on? After reviewing his experience and the time he had available for maintaining the speculative portfolio, Brian decided he felt most comfortable focusing on marketwide or industrywide movements. The primary reason was that he currently followed many sources that gave information on market or segment movements. By focusing on broad changes in the market or an industry, Brian could use information he felt reasonably comfortable with. Also, it was easy to maintain the base of information he needed to track his speculative portfolio. Given Brian's desire to focus on a "big picture," there were two alternatives that would allow him to transfer his predictions into investment action—index futures and index options.

According to some of Brian's friends, index futures provide significant opportunities for profit. However, these opportunities are accompanied by a significant amount of risk. A futures contract requires a commitment to buy or sell the underlying index some time in the future at a price agreed upon today. If Brian believes that the index value will fall in the near future, he could agree to sell a futures contract on the index. If the price of the index declines, he can repurchase his contract at a lower price and realize a profit. However, if the index price increases, his potential loss is theoretically unlimited.

Since Brian wants to limit his risk to $2,000, this potential liability is disturbing. The last thing he wants to do is to use funds from his portfolio to cover a speculative bet that has gone sour. Trading index futures would also be difficult since his initial investment is small. Most brokers won't accept a futures account of less than $10,000. Given his concern about potential liability and his limited initial investment, Brian turns to the final alternative, index options.

Stock index options are an ideal speculative vehicle in Brian's situation. The initial investment is relatively small, the level of risk can be managed effectively, and the necessary information for initiating and maintaining an account is provided by sources Brian already follows. Brian can also apply his previous experience with stock options to index option trading. Due to this similarity, the start-up costs of learning about trading stock index options should be minimal.

After reading more about stock index options, Brian decides that he has to make two more choices: which index to use and what specific strategy to employ. Brian limits himself to indexes reported in *The Wall Street Journal* and that have fairly significant trading volume. Brian's list of possibilities is shown in Exhibit 5-3.

Exhibit 5-3
High-Volume Optionable Indexes

NYSE Index
Major Market Index
S&P 100 Index
S&P 500 Index

Brian selects the S&P 100 as the best index for his purposes. He wants to speculate on marketwide changes, and the S&P 100 is a good proxy for the market. He also wants significant daily volume to lessen liquidity risk. This is no problem with the S&P 100, thousands of contracts are traded daily. Now that he has selected the index, Brian must determine the specific strategy he will use.

Brian could use several speculative strategies, summarized in Exhibit 5-4, depending on his expectations about short-term market movements.

Exhibit 5-4
Speculative Strategies

Buy Calls or Puts
Buy Straddle
Sell Straddle
Buy Strangle
Sell Strangle
Vertical Spreads
Horizontal Spreads
Long Butterfly
Short Butterfly

Brian feels that the market is poised for a fairly significant upward movement after several weeks of relative stability. Of the strategies available for taking advantage of a market increase, Brian selects purchasing call options. This seems most logical given his market expectation. Also, he feels more comfortable using a relatively simple strategy in his first transaction.

Now that Brian has selected both the index and the strategy, he must select a specific option. *The Wall Street Journal* listings for the S&P 100 are listed in Exhibit 5-5.

Exhibit 5-5
S&P 100 Index Listing

Strike	1-month	2-months	3-months
200	r	r	r
205	16 7/8	18 1/8	18 7/8
210	13 3/8	14 1/4	15 1/2
215	7 7/16	8 3/4	10
220	1 11/16	5 1/2	7 1/2
225	1/2	4	6 1/2
230	1/16	1 5/8	3 1/4
235	r	7/16	1 3/4
240	r	1/8	7/8
245	r	r	1/16

Index = 221.47
r = not traded

The current index value is 221.47. Call options with 10 different strike prices and three different maturities are listed for the S&P 100. This gives Brian 30 alternatives. Looking through the premiums required for each option, Brian eliminates those with strike prices below 225 (in the money) as too expensive. Options that are way out of the money don't appeal to Brian either because of the short time frame of the investment. The maximum available maturity is three months. If the market continues to be stable, these options will rapidly decay in value.

Brian decides to purchase five 225 calls that mature in two months for a premium of $400 each. This option was selected because it is slightly out of the money and has a maturity he feels comfortable with. Brian thinks options that are slightly out-of-the-money fit with his risk-return preference. The premiums on these options are all time value, so profit potential is better than it is with in-the-money options. Also the strike price is close to the current index value, so the risk is lower than with a way out-of-the-money option.

The two-month maturity was selected because Brian expects the market to move within a month. If this happens, his option will increase in value because the index will increase. The time-value decay of his option will not be as severe as it would be with a one-month option. And the premium is lower than on a three-month option.

Armed with this strategy, Brian calls his broker and executes the transaction summarized in Exhibit 5-6.

Exhibit 5-6
Transaction Summary

Order: Buy 5 nov 225 OEX call options at market ($4.00 each)
Call Back: Order Confirmed; Account credited for $2,000 plus commission.

Now that his strategy has been executed, Brian begins his maintenance program. This simply involves tracking his position in *The Wall Street Journal* every day and following other market information sources to update his opinion about expected market movements.

One week after Brian's purchase of the 225 calls, the S & P index has risen to 227.64. The premium on the 225 options has increased to $725. Brian's strategy worked well, if not sooner than he anticipated. Encouraged by this success, Brian stays with his strategy. Over the next three weeks, the index fluctuates around 228. During this time, the value of his options slowly declines as they approach maturity. Just over one month after his initial purchase, Brian decides to sell his options when the index value is at 228.14. The premium on his options is $512.50. His total profit for his first speculation is $522.50, $112.50 profit for each option times five options less a $40 commission. This means a return of about 26 percent for the month.

ANALYSIS

You may be left with a feeling that Brian Chadwick's success can be traced mostly to luck. Let us examine his method and determine whether such an assumption is valid.

The first phase of Brian's plan involved identifying how much he could use for speculation and an appropriate investment vehicle. His reasoning in choosing the amount was sound; $2,000 represents a small portion of Brian's total holdings. Also, the $1,000 left in his money market account is a reserve fund for the speculation. Brian consciously asked himself what he could *really* afford to lose. This is a key step in speculation. Rule number one is only speculate with money you can afford to lose. Brian's reasoning in selecting an investment vehicle was also good. He constructed a list of reasonable alternatives and pared the list down to a few choices that he felt comfortable with. Selection of the specific instrument was determined by the nature of the "bet" he wanted to make and the risk-return trade-off he was willing to assume.

Brian selected the index and speculation technique based on the market movement he anticipated. Since he felt comfortable betting on a market rise in the near term, the S&P 100 index was an appropriate choice. His concern about liquidity was also well founded. Lack of volume can be a significant problem. Brian also assumed that the premium quoted in *The Wall Street Journal* is a fairly accurate indicator of value. In less active markets, the published price may not reflect the current premium.

The choice of a call purchase was accurate given Brian's market expectation. However, he dismissed other strategies, namely spreads, because he thought they were complicated. This may have been a hasty decision. With Brian's market expectation, the riskiest strategy is a straight purchase of call options. If the index value had declined, he would have suffered a significant loss. Even more important, from a planning perspective, his investment is decaying from the day he enters the transaction. The market (index) must rise in a very short time for Brian to make money on index calls. More consideration of other strategies may have resulted in a different choice. Instead Brian made a transaction. This is a common mistake made by novice speculators.

Brian missed a few steps in the speculation guidelines listed in Exhibit 5-7. First, Brian made the investment without taking a few "dry runs." Because he didn't practice the strategy on paper, Brian increased his risk.

Exhibit 5-7
Speculation Guidelines

1. Never speculate when you are optimistic, only when you are confident.

2. Make your exit decision before you invest.

3. Build in flexibility.

4. You don't have to invest.

5. Practice before you preach.

Even though he had experience with stock options, some differences between this instrument and index options would have been highlighted in a practice session. The index may not correlate well with the information Brian is following, so he may be betting on the wrong index. Brian's portfolio is blue-chip stocks. If he had practiced his performance on paper, he might have discovered that the Major Market Index tracks the information base he uses more closely that the S&P index he invested in.

The other important error Brian made was investing without a clear idea of when he would exit the position. This is particularly important with index options. The value of an option declines as it approaches maturity, so the longer you wait to exit, the riskier the investment. In Brian's case, the lack of a clear exit goal cost him dearly, even though he ended up with a nice profit.

Brian should have had predetermined exit guidelines based on the index value or returns. For example, before entering the transaction, he could have decided to sell his options when the index value reached 227 or decreased to 220 before a certain date. Or he could have stated his decision in terms of return, exit when a 30 percent profit is achieved or a 10 percent loss is incurred. (Setting such limits is influenced by the risk of the particular strategy and may be refined by practicing the investment on paper.)

Brian Chadwick did a lot of things right. But he must become more disciplined if he wants to avoid significant losses in the future when his predictions may not be as good.

STEVE TYSON

Steve Tyson, who is approaching retirement, has been accumulating savings and investing them in the stock market for many years. He has always been a cautious investor, and is even more so at this point in his life—his primary investment goal is protecting what he has accumulated without sacrificing the opportunities to profit from a good economy. He has therefore resisted investing in vehicles such as certificates of deposit. He believes this strategy protects the value of his portfolio from deterioration through inflation.

Since Steve wants to protect his portfolio, he has decided to investigate the use of stock index options in conjunction with his portfolio in a hedging program. After reviewing some information on index options, Steve begins to construct a hedging program.

The first step in Steve's approach is to list the current holdings in his portfolio, shown in Exhibit 5-8.

Exhibit 5-8

Stock	Value
Burlington Northern	$ 15,900
Commonwealth Edison	14,325
Exxon	12,210
General Motors	14,980
Southern Cal. Edison	24,750
Pacific G & E	13,190
Navistar	18,560
Phillip Morris	10,830
DuPont	17,300
Philadelphia Electric	20,100
Detroit Edison	13,460
Portfolio Value	$175,605
Portfolio Beta 1.0	

Steve's portfolio is highly concentrated in blue-chip stocks with a limited investment in utilities. The overall beta is 1.0. Thus, Steve's portfolio is approximately as volatile as a portfolio of all stocks in the market.

Steve realizes that his hedging program will depend on how well an optionable index correlates with his portfolio. Given his holdings, Steve determines that the Major Market, S&P 100, S&P 500, NYSE Composite, or Value Line Composite will probably correlate best with his portfolio. To determine the correlation coefficient, he calculates weekly returns for his portfolio and those indexes over the last six months using *The Wall Street Journal* and calculates correlation coefficients between each index and his portfolio using his Hewlett-Packard 12-C. The results of these calculations are shown in Exhibit 5-9.

Exhibit 5-9
Correlation Coefficients

Index	Correlation with Portfolio
Major Market Index	.951
S&P 100	.898
S&P 500	.887
NYSE Composite	.865
Value Line Composite	.852

The index that correlates best with his portfolio over the last six months is the Major Market Index. Based on this information, Steve decides to try some practice hedges for the next month.

Since his primary motivation is to protect against portfolio declines, Steve is only going to consider using protective puts in the hedging program. The current level of the MMI is 341.91. The total value of his portfolio is $175,000. Since the beta of the portfolio is 1.0 and the contract value of each option is 100 times the current level ($34,191), he will purchase five put options (5 × $34,101 = $170,955) to approximate the value of his holdings. The current options available are listed in Exhibit 5-10.

Exhibit 5-10
Major Market Index Options

Strike	1-month	2-months	3-months
320	r	1/16	1/8
325	r	1/8	3/8
330	11/16	2 1/8	2 7/8
335	2 1/8	3 348	5 7/8
340	5 11/16	8 1/2	10 1/2
345	9 1/2	11 3/8	13 1/2
350	r	r	r

Index = 341.91
r = not traded

The only decisions remaining before Steve tries a practice transaction are selecting the option strike and maturity. Steve immediately ruled out maturities of more than one month because of the high premiums needed to buy these puts. The 330 strike put option appealed to Steve since it would protect him against any decline greater than about 4 percent with a fairly low premium of $68.75 per option. The total cost of insuring his $175,000 portfolio against a loss greater than 4 percent for one month would be $343.75. If this was a stable cost for one month's protection and the hedge was continuous, the return forgone by protecting the portfolio would be $343.75 times 12 months, or $4,125 divided by the value of the portfolio, $175,000, to equal 2.36 percent cost of insurance, plus commissions.

The practice hedge of five 330 MMI put options was tracked for one month. At the end of the month, the value of the Major Market Index equaled 354.48, a 3.68 percent increase from the previous month. Over the same time, the value of Steve's portfolio increased to $180,125, or approximately 3 percent. The put options expired worthless and Steve lost the $343.75 premium on the put options, so the total value of his portfolio was $179,781 at the end of the month. The market had increased over the month, and Steve's portfolio increased as well.

Steve was satisfied with the performance of his hedge. Even though he had to forego some profit, he was protected from a catastrophic loss by the hedge. His portfolio had shared in a nice gain over the month and he had peace of mind. Beginning the next month, Steve decided to initiate a permanent hedging strategy using index put options.

ANALYSIS

Steve Tyson's approach to protecting his portfolio is generally well conceived. Realizing that his main goal at this stage in his life is to protect what he has accumulated, he tested a realistic program for preserving that value. He avoided the temptation to sell his stocks and invest in fixed-income securities recognizing, rightly so, that unexpected inflation could be a serious threat to the purchasing power of his holdings. By maintaining a stock portfolio with a conservative hedging program, Steve can benefit from the growth of stock and protect his investment from significant losses.

Since his concept is sound, Steve executes his plan. The first stage is the most critical. He must locate an optionable index that correlates with his portfolio. The Major Market Index fits this criterion, but doesn't provide complete protection. There is a flaw in Steve's analysis. If the value of Steve's portfolio should fall, but the Major Market Index rises (which is a possibility because the correlation coefficient is less than 1.0) Steve will suffer a loss on both the portfolio *and* the options. As a result, he would lose more with the hedging program than from an unhedged position.

Another problem is that Steve is only concerned about catastrophic loss. His hedge only offsets losses (assuming perfect correlation) when the index value declines by about 4 percent. A 4 percent decline in a month is not only catastrophic but also rare. Steve's hedge provides no protection against a continuous decline of 3 percent per month, which is also very bad. In the second situation, the value of his portfolio is declining and he is paying for insurance that doesn't cover his loss. If he wants to increase his protection, all he has to do is buy puts with strike prices closer to the index value.

However, this can be very expensive since these options sell for higher premiums.

Steve has a good hedging program outlined. He is probably under-stating the risk of low correlation between his portfolio and the optionable index. He is also focusing his protection on avoiding huge losses. While this is a perfectly acceptable approach, he should not feel any tremendous peace of mind. He has protected himself against a particular type of risk (catastrophic loss), but, by purchasing out-of-the-money puts has increased his exposure to a market that suffers a slow, steady decline.

Chapter
Six

SIMULATIONS

This chapter is intended to improve your ability to recognize and use the stock index option techniques discussed in previous chapters. You will be required to make several decisions at key points in the simulation. Hopefully, this will help you gain experience to successfully use stock index options in your own portfolio. Before you proceed you should have a pencil and paper and a calculator handy. Solutions for these simulations are provided in Appendix E at the end of the book.

To effectively emphasize the key points in the simulations we must make some assumptions about your investment goals. These assumptions will allow us to analyze the situations in greater detail. Hopefully, the goals will be similar to your own. If they are not, you can modify the objectives to your own tastes given the conceptual framework described. For now, if the stated objectives are not aligned with your own, suppose you are advising a friend who has these goals.

SPECULATION SIMULATION

The first step in a speculative investment program is determining how much money you can risk. This amount is determined by the size of your current holdings as well as your expected income. For this simulation, suppose that you have $3,000 to commit to a speculative trading program. Remember, this is money that you can afford to lose if things don't go as expected.

Using information from several published sources, you decide that the market is poised for a major change, but you are uncertain about the direction. Several key announcements are expected in the next week concerning the outlook for the economy and interest rates. You would like to take advantage of the effect this new information will probably have on stock prices. Since you follow the Dow Jones Industrial Average in the news sources, you feel most comfortable speculating on the Major Market Index, a proxy for the DJIA. The current options and Major Market Index options and their premiums are listed in Exhibit 6-1.

Exhibit 6-1
Major Market Index Options

	Calls			Puts		
Strike	1-month	2-months	3-months	1-month	2-months	3-months
380	r	r	r	1/16	5/8	1 3/4
385	31 1/2	37	r	1/16	1	2 1/4
390	29	28 1/2	r	1/8	2 1/8	4
400	23 1/4	25 1/2	30 3/4	3/16	3 13/16	5
405	17 1/4	22 1/2	r	5/16	3 7/8	6
410	13	18 3/4	r	5/8	5	8 1/4
415	9	15 1/2	r	1/8	6 7/8	9 3/4
420	5 7/8	12 1/2	16 3/4	2 7/8	9 1/4	11 3/8
425	3 1/4	9 7/8	13	5 3/8	11 5/8	r
430	1 1/2	7 1/2	10 7/8	9	14 1/4	r
435	9/16	5 3/4	9 1/4	15 3/4	r	r
440	1/4	4	7 7/8	r	r	r
445	1/8	3	4 3/4	r	r	r

Index Value = 421.56
r = not traded

QUESTION #1—You expect a change in the market but are uncertain about the direction, what are your alternative speculative investments?

Describe your position on a piece of paper in specific terms. Be sure and list the option type, strike, premium, and maturity. Calculate the total investment in the position by determining the amount of premium paid or received from each option.

QUESTION #2—What is the total investment in this position? What is the maximum profit and loss from this technique?

QUESTION #3—What is your exit decision? Be specific.

Three days later, the Major Market Index options has changed as shown in Exhibit 6-2. Your expectations about the market remain unchanged for the time being.

Exhibit 6-2
Major Market Index Options
(Three days later)

Strike	Calls			Puts		
	1-month	2-months	3-months	1-month	2-months	3-months
380	54	52	r	r	r	r
385	46	49	r	r	7/16	1 3/16
390	44 1/2	43	r	r	9 1/16	1 9/16
400	34	34	r	1/16	1 1/8	2 1/2
405	28	31 1/2	30 3/4	1/16	1 3/4	3 7/8
410	22 1/2	25 1/2	28 1/2	1/16	2 1/2	4 5/8
415	17 5/8	21 1/2	24	1/16	3 1/2	5 3/4
420	12 5/8	18	22	1/16	4 5/8	7 3/4
425	7 7/8	16	18	5/16	6 1/2	10 5/8
430	4 1/8	12 1/2	16	1 1/2	9	12 1/4
435	1 1/4	9 5/8	14	3 7/8	11 1/2	r
440	1/4	7 5/8	11 3/4	r	r	r
445	1/16	5 1/2	9 3/4	r	r	r

Index Value = 432.65
r = not traded

QUESTION #4—What is the profit/loss on your position now? Have you reached an exit point yet?

The listing for Major Market Index options one week after the transaction was initiated are shown in Exhibit 6-3.

Exhibit 6-3
Major Market Index Options
(One week later)

Strike	Calls			Puts		
	1-month	2-months	3-months	1-month	2-months	3-months
380	r	r	r	1/8	7/8	r
385	r	r	r	1/8	r	r
390	38	r	r	7/16	2 1/16	r
400	33 1/2	r	r	3/4	2 5/8	r
405	30	r	r	1 1/4	3 1/4	r
410	24 1/2	r	r	1 15/16	4 7/8	r
415	16 1/2	20 1/4	r	4 3/8	7 3/4	9 7/8
420	13 1/2	16	r	6	9 3/4	11 3/4
425	10 1/2	14 3/4	r	8 3/8	11 3/4	14 7/8
430	8	12 1/2	r	11 3/8	14 3/8	18 1/4
435	5 7/8	10 3/4	13 1/2	13 5/8	17 1/4	r
440	4 1/4	8 3/8	11	16 3/4	20 1/2	r
445	2 7/8	6 5/8	9 1/8	19 1/4	r	r

Index Value = 426.04
r = not traded

At this point, you change to "no market opinion" because you do not feel comfortable making a prediction on the market now. Thus, you decide to get out of your current market position.

QUESTION #5—Describe how you would get out of your speculative position.

QUESTION #6—What is the profit/loss on your position now?

This was one example of applying a speculative position given a specific market opinion. Go back to the beginning of this simulation and repeat the questions assuming that you forecast a slight market increase and a slight market decline. These three scenarios provide a sample of the situations speculators frequently encounter. Practicing with your own set of expectations after you complete this simulation should improve your chances at being a successful speculator.

HEDGING SIMULATION

Suppose you own the portfolio listed in Exhibit 6-4.

Exhibit 6-4

Stock	Value	Beta
Chrysler	$ 12,350	1.25
General Motors	15,675	1.10
Navistar	6,545	1.00
Chicago Pacific	9,875	0.60
Maytag	13,240	0.90
Boston Edison	20,800	0.60
Damon Corp.	14,100	1.30
Johnson & Johnson	27,300	1.00
Pennzoil	18,750	0.90
Standard Oil	18,000	1.10
American Standard	7,900	1.15
Hewlett-Packard	22,255	1.30
IBM	10,250	1.75
Bristol-Myers	15,500	1.00

QUESTION #1—What is the beta for the total portfolio listed in Exhibit 6-4? What information is provided by a portfolio beta?

Your primary objective is to protect the value of the portfolio without foregoing profits if prices rise. By insuring your portfolio against potential short-term market declines you are hoping to increase your long-term return.

QUESTION #2—What hedging strategies are available for an individual with these goals? Which strategy would you recommend?

The weekly returns for your portfolio over the last six months are listed in Exhibit 6-5. Weekly returns for some of the major optionable indexes are listed in Exhibit 6-6. These returns were obtained from *The Wall Street Journal* for the previous six months.

Exhibit 6-5
Weekly Portfolio Returns

Week	Return
1	.31%
2	.45
3	−.07
4	−.12
5	.21
6	.30
7	−.22
8	.09
9	.07
10	.41
11	−.16
12	.11
13	.06
14	.00
15	−.05
16	−.31
17	.09
18	.31
19	.21
20	.02
21	−.16
22	−.09
23	.33
24	.07
25	.11
26	−.14

Exhibit 6-6
Weekly Index Returns

Week	S&P100	S&P500	MMI
1	.21%	.23%	.36%
2	.38	.46	.40
3	.02	−.03	−.10
4	−.10	−.06	−.02
5	.25	.18	.45
6	.28	.16	.30
7	−.20	−.20	−.32
8	.00	−.02	−.18
9	.05	.03	.10
10	.25	.18	.11
11	.01	.09	.07
12	−.02	.00	.06
13	.10	.08	.22
14	−.08	−.06	−.21
15	−.05	−.02	−.11
16	−.29	−.21	−.40
17	.15	.16	.28
18	.16	.13	.24
19	.31	.24	.18
20	−.10	−.06	−.01
21	−.21	−.18	−.28
22	.03	.02	.11
23	.13	.08	.22
24	.13	.04	.26
25	.03	.09	.18
26	−.12	−.04	.01

QUESTION #3—What is the correlation coefficient between the returns from each index and the portfolio? What does this statistic indicate? Which index, if any, would be the best to use in a hedging program?

Now that you have determined the portfolio beta and the index that has the highest correlation with the portfolio, you must identify the specific option to be used in the hedging program. The current listing of stock index option premiums is shown in Exhibit 6-7.

QUESTION #4—How many options should be used to hedge the portfolio? Why?

QUESTION #5—Which option (call or put; strike price; maturity) should be used to hedge the portfolio given your stated objectives? What are the trade-offs involved in using options with higher or lower strike prices and shorter or longer maturities?

QUESTION #6—Are there any other factors that should be considered before entering a transaction?

Suppose that you initiate a hedging transaction based on the information used above. Now you should be concerned about obtaining information on both your portfolio and the hedge. You should follow the performance of your position on a daily basis through *The Wall Street Journal*.

QUESTION #7—Under what circumstances would you remove the hedge? Why? Would it ever be advisable to remove the hedge if the market began to decline?

Exhibit 6-8 lists options prices and the portfolio value two weeks after the hedging transaction was initiated.

QUESTION #8—If you closed out your position right now, what would your total profit/loss be on the hedged portfolio? If the portfolio was unhedged, what would your total profit/loss be?

QUESTION #9—What tax implications would be associated with closing this position? Why?

These simulations should have helped you overcome the uncertainties associated with applying the techniques described earlier. Now that you have worked through these simulations, you should practice hedging or speculating, depending on your goal. Use the questions in the simulations as a guide for your own program and you will increase your chances of success.

Exhibit 6-7
Stock Index Option Premiums

Chicago Board

S&P 100 INDEX

Strike	Calls—Last			Puts—Last		
Price	Dec	Jan	Feb	Dec	Jan	Feb
205	33½	...	...	1/16	1/16	...
210	29½	28	...	1/16	⅛	9/16
215	...	23	...	1/16	⅜	13/16
220	19⅞	20⅝	19⅛	1/16	⅝	1 7/16
225	14¾	15½	15¾	3/16	1¼	2 7/16
230	9⅝	11½	13	½	2¼	3¾
235	5	7⅝	9½	1 7/16	4⅛	5½
240	29½	28	...	1/16	⅛	9/16
245	⅞	2⅝	4⅛	1/16	⅝	1 7/16
250	3/16	1½	2⅛	1/16	11¼	1 7/16
255	...	11/16	1 11/16	...	18	...

Total call volume 192,517 Total call open int. 527,341
Total put volume 132,826 Total put open int. 830,472
The index: High 239,26; Low 236,57; Close 238,78 +1,86.

S&P 500 INDEX

Strike	Calls—Last			Puts—Last		
Price	Dec	Jan	Feb	Dec	Jan	Feb
215	...	...	...	...	...	...
220	32	...	...	...	...	...
225	...	...	...	...	¼	...
230	20½	...	22½	1/16	½	1¾
235	17⅛	18	...	3/16	15/16	2⅜
240	11⅜	...	...	⅜	1¾	4
245	6¾	10	12½	1	2⅞	5¾
250	3½	6¼	9⅜	2⅜	4¾	7
255	1⅜	4⅛	7	5¾	7¼	10½
260	⅜	2	...	...	...	...
265	...	...	...	...	19⅛	...

Total call volume 7.522 Total call open int. 105.456
Total put volume 6.963 Total put open int. 86.154
The index: High 251.53; Low 248.94; Close 250.96 +1.68.

American Exchange

MAJOR MARKET INDEX

Strike	Calls—Last			Puts—Last		
Price	Dec	Jan	Feb	Dec	Jan	Feb
315	56	...	...	...	...	...
325	...	...	...	1/16	3/16	...
330	...	...	...	...	3/16	...
335	36	...	...	1/16	½	1
340	...	...	...	1/16	9/16	2⅛
345	26¼	...	...	⅛	1 1/16	2⅞
350	24½	...	...	3/16	1⅝	3⅜
355	20¼	21¾	...	7/16	2 7/16	4⅜

Total call volume 29,3897 Total call open int. 74,279
Total put volume 26,537 Total put open int. 104,052
The index: High 374,35; Low 369,46; Close 373,33 +3,23.

OIL INDEX

Strike	Calls—Last			Puts—Last		
Price	Dec	Jan	Feb	Dec	Jan	Feb
140	...	...	9⅝	...	...	...
145	4	5⅜	...	...	...	...
150	17/16	2¾	...	2½	...	...
155	5/16	1¾	...	...	...	...

Total call volume 300 Total call open int. 3.055
Total put volume 5 Total put open int. 737
The index: High 148.72; Low 146.08; Close 148.33, +2.05.

INSTITUTIONAL INDEX

Strike	Calls—Last			Puts—Last		
Price	Dec	Jan	Feb	Dec	Jan	Feb
225	...	...	...	...	3/16	...
235	20	28	...	...	11/16	...
240	15	...	...	¼	1 5/16	...
245	9⅞	...	...	¾	2¾	...
250	5¼	7⅔	9½	1 3/16	3¾	6¼
255	2¼	...	6½	3	5¾	...
260	11/16	2 9/16	...	6¾	...	...
270	...	...	...	16¾	17⅞	...

Total call volume 5.022 Total call open int. 28.314
Total put volume 1.385 Total put open int. 25.439
The index: High 254.10; Low 251.16; Close 253.58 +2.03.

Philadelphia Exchange

GOLD/SILVER INDEX

Strike	Calls—Last			Puts—Last		
Price	Dec	Jan	Feb	Dec	Jan	Feb
65	12	...	...	...	...	...
70	3	...	...	1/16	⅛	...
75	...	...	...	¾	2 3/16	3¼
80	¾	2½	...	3¼	...	...

Total call volume 151 Total cost open int. 1,809
Total put volume 92 Total put open int. 2.707
The index: High 77.67; Low 76.28; Close 76.70 +0.56.

VALUE LINE INDEX OPTIONS

Strike	Calls—Last			Puts—Last		
Price	Dec	Jan	Feb	Dec	Jan	Feb
215	19¼	...	...	1/16	...	...
220	14¼	...	...	⅛	...	...
225	8½	...	...	⅜	2½	...
230	4	6⅞	...	1⅜	...	...
235	1⅜	3¾	...	4	...	...

Total call volume 1,102 Total call open int. 9,212
Total put volume 412 Total put open int. 6.376
The index: High 231.72; Low 230.54; Close 231.40 +0.58.

NATIONAL O-T-C INDEX

Strike	Calls—Last			Puts—Last		
Price	Dec	Jan	Feb	Dec	Jan	Feb
215	3¼	...	...	...	...	...
220	...	3¾	...	3¾	...	...

Total call volume 151 Total call open int. 1,102
Total put volume 2 Total put open int. 1.264
The index: High 216.10; Low 215.21; Close 215.68 +0.13.

N.Y. Stock Exchange

NYSE INDEX OPTIONS

Strike	Calls—Last			Puts—Last		
Price	Dec	Jan	Feb	Dec	Jan	Feb
125	...	...	...	...	...	¼
130	...	...	...	...	¼	9/16
132½	...	...	...	...	¼	...
135	9¾	...	...	⅛	⅝	1 5/16
137½	...	...	...	3/16	1 1/16	...
140	5	5¾	6¼	½	¼	2¾

Total call volume 5,288 Total call open int. 23,874
Total put volume 4,009 Total put open int. 37.971
The index: High 143.72; Low 142.39; Close 143.46 +0.89.

NYSE BETA INDEX

Strike	Calls—Last			Puts—Last		
Price	Dec	Jan	Feb	Dec	Jan	Feb
290	20¾	...	...	...	...	...
295	15½	...	...	⅜	...	...
300	11¼	...	...	...	...	...
305	8	10¼	...	1 7/16	...	...
310	4¾	7½	...	3¼	7¾	...

Total call volume 124 Total call open int. 947
Total put volume 163 Total put open int. 1,110
The index: High 310.96; Low 306.31; Close 310.15 +1.56.

Pacific Exchange

TECHNOLOGY INDEX

Strike	Calls—Last			Puts—Last		
Price	Dec	Jan	Feb	Dec	Jan	Feb
115	...	...	7¼	2½	...	...

Total call volume 60 Total call open int. 75
Total put volume 102 Total put open int. 33
The index: High 116.56; Low 115.97; Close 116.51 +0.32.

FINANCIAL NEWS COMPOSITE INDEX

Strike	Calls—Last			Puts—Last		
Price	Dec	Jan	Feb	Dec	Jan	Feb
155	20¾	...	...	...	...	...
160	15½	...	...	...	...	...
165	...	...	...	...	1 1/16	...
170	5¾	6¾	...	9/16	2	...
175	2¼	4¼	...	2¼	4¼	...

Total call volume 1,060 Total call open int. 7,658
Total put volume 417 Total put open int. 7,291
The index: High 117.29; Low 173.18; Close 174.85 +1.45.

Exhibit 6-8
Stock Index Option Premiums
(Two Weeks Later)

Chicago Board

S&P 100 INDEX

Strike		Calls—Last			Puts—Last	
Price	Dec	Jan	Feb	Dec	Jan	Feb
205	33½	...	...	1/16	...	...
210	28¼	27½	28¼	⅛	⅜	11/16
215	23	23	...	⅛	½	1
220	18¼	18¾	19⅝	¼	11/16	1⅞
225	13½	14⅜	15⅜	⅜	2	3
230	9	10¾	11⅞	1½	3⅝	4½
235	5⅜	7⅝	9⅛	3¼	5⅜	6½
240	2 15/16	5	6¾	5¾	7⅞	8¾
245	1 3/16	3	4⅜	9¾	10⅞	...
250	7/16	1⅝	2 11/16	13¾	10⅞	...
255	½	⅞	1 11/16	...	...	...

Total call volume 98.967 Total call open int. 532.680
Total put volume 99.108 Total put open int. 894,394
The index: High 238,46; Low 236,12; Close 237,10 –1,41.

S&P 500 INDEX

Strike		Calls—Last			Puts—Last	
Price	Dec	Jan	Feb	Dec	Jan	Feb
215	...	...	...	...	...	5/16
220	...	...	...	...	...	11/16
225	...	...	...	1/16	...	...
230	18⅝	...	...	3/16	...	...
235	...	...	...	½	...	2¾
240	10¼	...	13¼	1¼	...	4
245	6½	...	...	2¾	...	6
250	3⅝	5⅞	7⅜	7⅞	...	8
255	1⅜	3⅜	...	7⅞	...	...
260	⅜	...	3½	...	...	...
265	3/16	...	2¼	...	...	...

Total call volume 4,006 Total call open int. 102,195
Total put volume 2,109 Total put open int. 94,581
The index: High 249,73; Low 247,45; Close 248,75 –0.98.

American Exchange

MAJOR MARKET INDEX

Strike		Calls—Last			Puts—Last	
Price	Dec	Jan	Feb	Dec	Jan	Feb
325	...	...	...	1/16	...	...
330	...	...	...	1/16	...	...
335	...	...	...	½	13/16	...
340	31¾	34½	...	3/16	1 3/16	...
345	27	...	...	5/16	1¾	...
350	23	24¾	...	11/16	2½	...
355	18	...	...	1¼	3¾	...

Total call volume 15,338 Total call open int. 80,250
Total put volume 9,414 Total put open int. 12,162
The index: High 371,45; Low 369,09; Close 370,54 +0,07.

OIL INDEX

Strike		Calls—Last			Puts—Last	
Price	Dec	Jan	Feb	Dec	Jan	Feb
135	18¾	...	...	...	...	
140	...	...	...	1/16	...	...
145	9½	...	...	...	...	...
150	5	...	...	1 7/16	...	...
155	2 5/16	3⅜	...	3¾	...	...
160	9/16	1 13/16	...	...	...	...

Total call volume 315 Total call open int. 2,701
Total put volume 95 Total put open int. 963
The index: High 154.14; Low 152.64; Close 153.91, +1.14.

INSTITUTIONAL INDEX

Strike		Calls—Last			Puts—Last	
Price	Dec	Jan	Feb	Dec	Jan	Feb
225	...	...	...	...	⅜	...
240	12½	...	...	13/16	...	⅜
245	8⅝	...	...	1¾	3⅞	...
250	5⅜	...	...	3⅜	5⅞	6⅜
255	3	...	...	6¼	...	...
260	1 5/16	...	...	...	...	...
265	½	...	...	...	...	...

Total call volume 1,415 Total call open int. 34,194
Total put volume 2,291 Total put open int. 47,114
The index: High 252,62; Low 250,74; Close 251.79 –0.90.

Philadelphia Exchange

GOLD/SILVER INDEX

Strike		Calls—Last			Puts—Last	
Price	Dec	Jan	Feb	Dec	Jan	Feb
65	...	...	...	...	7/16	...
70	...	...	...	9/16	1¼	...
75	3	...	...	1¾	3⅜	...
80	1⅜	2 11/16	...	4½	6½	...
85	⅜	1 1/16	2½	...	...	...

Total call volume 110 Total cost open int. 831
Total put volume 78 Total put open int. 874
The index: High 77.24; Low 75.68; Close 76.20 –0.13.

VALUE LINE INDEX OPTIONS

Strike		Calls—Last			Puts—Last	
Price	Dec	Jan	Feb	Dec	Jan	Feb
210	...	...	...	...	...	1⅛
215	...	...	...	¼	1 3/16	2⅛
220	12⅛	...	...	¾	2⅛	...
225	7¾	...	...	1⅞	4	...
230	4½8	...	7⅞	4	...	...
235	2⅛	...	...	...	...	...
240	¾	2⅜	3¾	...	...	...

Total call volume 526 Total call open int. 1,748
Total put volume 278 Total put open int. 2,461
The index: High 230.94; Low 228.43; Close 229.98 –1.00.

N.Y. Stock Exchange

NYSE INDEX OPTIONS

Strike		Calls—Last			Puts—Last	
Price	Dec	Jan	Feb	Dec	Jan	Feb
130	...	...	...	⅛	9/16	⅞
132½	...	...	...	¼	...	...
135	...	...	9⅜	⅜	1 5/16	1 13/16
137½	5 11/16	...	...	¾	1 15/16	...
140	3⅝5	5⅛	6	1 9/16	2⅞	3⅝
145	1⅜	2⅝	3½	4	...	...
147½	11/16	...	...	6	...	...
150	5/16	1 3/16	1⅞	8⅜	...	...

Total call volume 1,471 Total call open int. 7,181
Total put volume 1,759 Total put open int. 10,428
The index: High 142.65; Low 141.31; Close 142.02 –0.63.

NYSE BETA INDEX

Strike		Calls—Last			Puts—Last	
Price	Dec	Jan	Feb	Dec	Jan	Feb
280	...	...	...	¾	1¼	...
285	...	...	...	...	1⅞	...
290	...	...	...	1¼	...	...
295	...	...	...	3	...	...
300	...	...	...	5	...	...
305	6	...	...	7¾	...	...
310	3½	...	...	...	...	...

Total call volume 49 Total call open int. 306
Total put volume 48 Total put open int. 394
The index: High 307.77; Low 304.02; Close 305.90 –1.87.

Pacific Exchange

TECHNOLOGY INDEX

Strike		Calls—Last			Puts—Last	
Price	Dec	Jan	Feb	Dec	Jan	Feb
115	...	...	5⅜	...	...	...

Total call volume 20 Total call open int. 194
Total put volume 0 Total put open int. 119
The index: High 114.94; Low 113.71; Close 114.24 –0.70.

FINANCIAL NEWS COMPOSITE INDEX

Strike		Calls—Last			Puts—Last	
Price	Dec	Jan	Feb	Dec	Jan	Feb
155	18½	...	...	...	...	...
160	...	...	...	3/16	...	...
165	8⅝	10	...	9/16	...	...
167½	7	...	...	1 5/16	...	...
170	4⅞	6½	...	1¾	3⅛	...
172½	3½	...	...	2¾	...	...
175	2⅜	...	4¼	5⅜	...	

Total call volume 1,776 Total call open int. 7,113
Total put volume 1,092 Total put open int. 10,135
The index: High 173.18; Low 171.52; Close 172.78 +0.05.

Appendix
A

GLOSSARY

AMERICAN OPTION—An option that may be exercised at any time prior to expiration.

AT-THE-MONEY OPTION—The strike price is equal to the market price.

BUTTERFLY SPREAD—Option strategy in which an investor sells two calls and buys two calls on the same or on different markets. This strategy assumes that the call contracts have different maturity dates.

CALL OPTION—A buyer has the right (but not necessarily the obligation) to buy 100 shares of the underlying security at a fixed price before a stated date—usually, three, six or nine months hence.

CASH SETTLEMENT—The settlement procedure for an index option is unusual in that no securities change hands. Settlements for index options contracts are in cash.

CHICAGO BOARD OPTIONS EXCHANGE (CBOE)—Formal options exchange where trading of the S&P 100 and S&P 500 Stock Index Options is conducted.

CONTRACT VALUE—The total value of a stock index option contract is $100 times the index value. If the S&P 500 index is 230, then the contract value would equal $23,000.

COVERED CALL WRITING—The writer of call options takes the opposite side of the market from the buyers of call options; in effect, the writer is "short" the market in that he expects the underlying stock to either stay at the same price or to decline in price. The writer owns the underlying shares of stock.

DAY ORDER—When an order is good for that day only. If the order is not filled by the close of trading that day, the order is automatically cancelled.

DEEP-IN-THE-MONEY—The exercise price of a call option is well below the price of the underlying security (stock).

DEEP-OUT-OF-THE-MONEY—The exercise price of a call option is well above the price of the underlying security (stock).

DIVERSIFICATION—Reducing or spreading risk by allocating assets to different classes of investments, e.g. combinations of stocks, bonds, options, futures, etc.

EUROPEAN OPTIONS—An option that may be exercised only on the last day of trading before expiration of the option.

EXERCISE PRICE—Exercise of "strike" prices are set at five point intervals. New strike prices are introduced as the index level advances or declines.

FLOOR BROKER—Individual who executes trades on the floor of the exchange on behalf of a client.

HEDGING—Typically an investment strategy used to offset or reduce risk.

HORIZONTAL SPREAD—Strategy involving the buying and selling of equal numbers of options contracts which have the same exercise price, although having different maturity dates. This is also known as a "calendar spread."

IN-THE-MONEY OPTION—Options that have an intrinsic value equal to the market price minus the strike price.

LIQUIDITY—An investor has the ability to convert an asset or security to cash without suffering a substantial loss at the time of sale. Typically, a stock with a great many shares outstanding is said to be "liquid."

LIMIT ORDER—Order to buy or sell at a stated price or better than the stated price.

MARGIN REQUIREMENTS—The minimum amount that an investor deposits with a brokerage, typically 50% of the purchase price of eligible securities of 50% of the proceeds of a short sale.

MARKET ORDER—Order to buy or sell at the prevailing market price.

MARKET-VALUE WEIGHTING—An index, the components of which are weighted to the market value of the outstanding shares of stock represented in the index.

NAKED OPTION—A call writer whereby the writer does not own the underlying common stock (see covered call option).

OPTIONS CLEARING CORPORATION (OCC)—A corporation, owned by the major stock exchanges, that issues all options contracts and guarantees that both parties to a trade fulfill their respective responsibilities.

OUT-OF-THE MONEY OPTION—Options that have no tangible intrinsic value because the market price is less than the strike price.

OPTION—The right, acquired for a consideration, to buy or sell an asset at a fixed price within a specified period of time.

PORTFOLIO—Total investment holdings; any combination of stocks, bonds, options, real estate and cash held by investors the total effect of which is to reduce risk.

POSITION LIMITS—Limits set on the number of contracts of each class than an option's investor can control. 15,000 contracts is the limit for index+options, on either side of the market.

PREMIUM—Each premium point is equal to $100. An option with a premium of 3⅝ would cost $362.50 to purchase (not including transactions costs).

PUT—An options contract by which the holder has the right to sell a specific number of shares at a specified price by a stated date.

SHORT SALE—An investment strategy used to take advantage of an expected decline in the price of a security whereby the investor sells a security or contract not owned by the seller.

SPECULATING—An investment strategy that assumes a higher than average degree of risk (possibility of loss) because of a higher than average possible gain.

SPREAD—The difference in prices of put and call options held by an investor on the same stock or index. The strike price and the expiration dates, in fact, may be different.

STOCK INDEX OPTION—An options contract on a broad-based measure of market activity which allows investors to take a position on the market as a whole, rather than on just one stock.

STOCK INDEX—A measure of stock market activity (performance) based on the average performance of the individual stocks contained in the index, e.g. S&P 100 Index.

STOP ORDER—Order to buy or sell once a specific market price is reached; commonly used to prevent excessive losses or to initiate automatically new positions.

STRADDLE—Investors holding an equal number of put and call options on the same stock or stock index; typically, all the contracts have the same strike price and the same maturity date.

SYSTEMATIC RISK—Changes in market or economic conditions, e.g. interest rates, energy prices and inflation, that effect all stocks in some degree.

UNCOVERED OPTION—The investor does not hold the underlying security in the event that delivery of the option contract is required; also known as a "naked" option.

UNSYSTEMATIC RISK—Company specific factors that affect the risk of holding a stock or other security, e.g. a strike, large government contract, and so forth. Unsystematic risk would tend not to be industry wide nor affect the economy as a whole.

VOLATILITY—A statistical measure (usually expressed as a standard deviation) or price movements of a stock.

VERTICAL SPREAD—Buying and selling two options with different strike price.

WRITER—An individual who sells options.

Appendix
B

Introduction to Options*

DESCRIPTION

The word *option* has many different meanings, but most of them include the ability or right to choose a certain alternative. One definition provided by Webster's dictionary is ''the right, acquired for a consideration, to buy or sell something at a fixed price within a specified period of time.'' This definition is very general and applies to puts, calls, warrants, real estate options, or any other contracts entered into between two parties in which a choice of action or decision can be put off for a limited time at a cost. The person acquiring the option pays an agreed upon amount of money providing the option. The seller of the option has committed to deliver a particular parcel of land or other good and valuable consideration for a specified time period at a specified price.

The seller of the option has given up the ability to sell that property to another buyer for the specified period of time.

Put options and *call options* pertain to the sale or purchase of common stock, respectively. A put is an option to sell 100 shares of common stock at a specified price at a given period of time for which the option buyer pays the writer or seller of the option a premium. This premium is also referred to as the *price* of the option. Call options are the opposite of put options and allow the owner the right to

*This material appeared originally in Geoffery Hirt, Stan Block, and Fred Jury, *The Investor's Desktop Portfolio Planner* (Chicago, IL: Probus Publishing Co., 1986). Reprinted with permission.

137

Table B-1
Newspaper Format for Options Quotations

Options & NY Close	Strike Price	Vol.	Last Price —Dec—	Vol.	Last Price —Mar—	Vol.	Last Price —Jun—
Ford	40	131	14⅜	56	14½		no trade
54⅛	Put 40		no trade	15	⅟₁₆		no trade
54⅛	45	1016	9⅜	48	9⅞	2	10⅜
54⅛	Put 45		no trade	29	¼	5	½
54⅛	50	2701	4⅜	127	5⅜	101	6⅛
54⅛	Put 50	586	⅛	100	1	7	1⅞
54⅛	55	550	¹³⁄₁₆	248	2¼	49	3
54⅛	Put 55	111	1⅛	32	3	3	3½
54⅛	60	60	⅛	82	¹¹⁄₁₆	61	1¼

buy 100 shares of common stock from the seller of the call option. The seller of an option contract, either a put of a call , is often referred to as the "writer" of the option contract.

Before investors can understand various option stategies, they must be able to comprehend what creates option prices. Investors should look at the Ford Motor example in Table B-1. Ford Motor common stock closed at 54.125 per share on the New York Stock Exchange on this day and the puts and calls are available at strike prices $40, $45, $50, $55. The December 50 call closed at 4⅜ ($437.50 for one call on 100 shares), while the December 55 call closed at 13/16. The $50 call is said to be "in-the-money" because of the market price $54.125 is above the strike price of $50. The $55 call is "out-of-the-money" since the strike price is above the market price.

"In-the-money" options have an intrinsic value equal to the market price minus the strike price. In the case of Ford Motor, December 50 call, the intrinsic value is $4.125, as indicated by the following formula:

$$\text{Market} - \text{Strike} = \text{Intrinsic Value}$$
$$\$54.125 - \$50.000 = \$4.125$$

Options that are "out-of-the-money" have no tangible intrinsic value. The Ford Motor December 55 call would have a negative

$.875 intrinsic value derived from the same formula. When the market price minus the strike price is negative, the negative value represents the amount the stock price must increase to have the option "at-the-money," where the strike price and market price are equal. Returning to the Ford Motor $50 December call, we see the total premium is 4⅜, while the intrinsic value is 4⅛. This call option has an additional premium of $¼ due to other factors. The total premium (option price) is a combination of the intrinsic value plus the speculative premium (which is a function of the common stock volatility and risk), time remaining until expiration of the option contract, dividend yield on the underlying common stock, potential leverage of the option contract, and market expectations of price changes in the common stock.

Generally speaking, the higher the volatility of a common stock, the greater will be the speculative premium in the options contracts. The longer the time remaining until expiration of the contract, the higher the speculative premium. The deeper the option is in the money, the smaller leverage potential and therefore the smaller the speculative premium for that option contract.

The speculative premium for any given company's option contracts may vary a great deal. Ford Motor speculative premiums are not very high, due to a relatively low volatility in the price of the common stock. Option premiums for companies that traditionally have had larger price changes in the market place, will be higher than Ford Motor's.

STRENGTHS

One of the strengths of an options contract is the ability to control 100 shares of common stock at a vastly reduced price. The leverage involved in an options contract can be very large. A very small percent change in the price of a common stock can cause a very large percentage change in the price of options contracts for the same company.

A second strength of an options contract is the ability to use either put or call options as a form of insurance for stocks already owned in an investor's portfolio. An investor may wish to purchase a put option contract should he or she feel the value of a particular stock in the portfolio may be subject to a substantial decline. The put option contract would give that investor the right to sell 100 shares of stock for a specified price for a set period of time.

WEAKNESSES

Weaknesses of options contracts include very volatile price movements, relatively high transaction costs, and a relatively short period of ownership.

UNIQUE FEATURES

One of the unique features for options investing is the ability to write a call option contract against an existing stock portfolio as a means of substantially enhancing the total income received from that portfolio. An investor who owns 100 shares of Exxon Corporation may elect to sell (or write) an option contract against the 100 shares of Exxon. For selling this contract the investor will receive the option price, sometimes referred to as "the premium," offered by the market place at a particular point in time. This premium that is received by the owner of Exxon is retained no matter what future events follow. If the price of Exxon goes down and the time period expires for the call option, the call writer retains the entire amount of the call premium. If the price of the stock goes up above the strike price of the option contract the call writer may have the stock called away but retains the premium originally paid for that option.

WHERE AND HOW TO BUY

The Chicago Board Options Exchange (CBOE) was established in 1973 as the first exchange for option contracts. The response from the investment community was overwhelming, and within three years the American, Pacific, and Philadelphia stock exchanges were also trading options contracts. By 1985 the list of stocks with available option contracts increased from the original list of 20 companies to over 390 companies.

Table B-2 displays a list of all companies with listed options traded on the Chicago Board Options Exchange. Other options exchanges trade equity options on additional stocks. All stock options are quoted daily in national business newspapers such as *Investor's Daily* or *The Wall Street Journal*.

The options contracts on individual common stocks are designed with a standardize three-, six-, and nine-month expiration dates. These expiration dates operate on three calendar cycles.

Table B-2
Companies with Options
Traded on the Chicago Board Options Exchange

Alcoa	Intern'l. Min. & Chem.
Amdahl	Intern'l. Paper
Amer. Electric Power	ITT
American Express	Jim Walter Corp.
Amer. Hosp. Supply	Johnson & Johnson
AMP	K Mart
Apache	Kerr McGee
AT&T	Lifemark
Atlantic Richfield	Litton Industries
Avon	Loral
Bally Mfg.	Mary Kay Cosmetics
BankAmerica	McDonald's
Baxter Labs	Medtronics
Bethlehem Steel	Merck
Black & Decker	Merrill Lynch
Boeing	Middle South Utilities
Boise Cascade	MMM
Bristol-Meyers	Mobil
Brunswick	Monsanto
Burlington Northern	NCR
Burroughs	Nat'l. Semiconductor
Captial Cities Comm.	Norfolk Southern
CBS	Northern Telecom
Celanese	Northrop
Cessna	Northwest Airlines
Champion Intern'l.	Northwest Industries
CIGNA	Occidental Petroleum
Citicorp	Owens-Illinois
Coastal	Paine Webber

B-2 Table (Continued)

Coca-Cola	Paradyne
Colgate-Palmolive	Pennzoil
Commonwealth Ed.	PepsiCo
Computer Sciences	Polaroid
Continental Illinois	Ralston Purina
Control Data	Raytheon
Corning Glass	RCA
Datapoint	Revlon
Delta Air Lines	R.J. Reynolds
Diabold	Rockwell Intern'l.
Digital Equipment	ROLM
Disney	Sabine
Dow Chemical	Safeway Stores
du Pont	Schlumberger
Eastman Kodak	Sears Roebuck
Eckerd (Jack)	Skyline
Edwards (A.G.)	Southern
Engelhard	Southern Pacific
Esmark	Southwest Airlines
Exxon	Sperry
Federal Express	Squibb
First Boston	Standard Oil (Ind.)
Fluor	Storage Technology
Ford	Superior Oil
Freeport McMoRan	Syntex
General Dynamics	Tandy
General Electric	Tektonix
General Foods	Teledyne
General Motors	Texas Instruments
Great Western Fin.	Tidewater
Gulf & Western	Toys "R" Us
Halliburton	UAL
Harris	United Technologies
Hewlett-Packard	Upjohn
Hitachi	Viacom Intern'l.
Holiday Inns	Wal-Mart Stores
Homestake Mining	Warner Comm.
Honeywell	Weyerhaeuser
Hughes Tool	Williams
Humana	Xerox
IBM	
Intern'l Flavors	
& Fragrances	

Companies may be added or deleted from this list at any time because of mergers, acquisitions, or other reasons. There are other options that may be trading on other options exchanges.

Some stocks trade during cycle one with expiration dates in January, April, July, and October. Cycle two is February, May, August, and November. Cycle three is March, June, September, and December.

As one month's expiration date comes up, another month in the cycle is added. For example, as the January option expires, the October nine-month option is added, and the cycle is continued. The use of three cycles spreads out the expiration dates for the options so that not all contracts come due on the same day. Any options positions approaching expiration must be closed out no later than the third Friday following the third Thursday of the month when the option is scheduled to expire.

The exercise price of an option contract is often referred to as the striking price of the contract. This is the fixed price at which the contract is specified for either sales or purchase. For all stocks priced under $100 per share the striking price changes by $5 intervals, and for stocks selling over $100 per share the strike price changes by $10 per share.

As the underlying stocks change price in the open market, options with new striking prices are added. For example, a stock selling at $30 per share when the January option is added will have a striking price of $30, but if the stock gets to $32.50 per share, which is half-way to the next striking price, the options exchange may add another option with a $35 strike price.

This standardization of expiration dates and strike prices creates more certainty when buying and selling options in a changing market and allows more efficient trading strategies because of better coordination between stock prices, striking prices, and expiration dates. Dividend payments by the companies involved do not affect the option contract. Transactions in option contracts occur at arm's length between buyer and seller without any matchmaking needed on the part of an individual stock broker.

OPTIONS CLEARING CORPORATION

All options transactions are governed by the Options Clearing Corporation. Much of the liquidity and ease of operation of all of the options exchanges is due to the role of the Options Clearing Corporation. The Options Clearing Corporation functions as the issuer of all option contracts listed on the major option exchanges. Investors who want to trade puts and calls need to have an approved account with brokerage firm. Upon opening the account, the investor will receive a prospectus from the Options Clearing Corporation detailing all aspects of options trading.

Options are bought and sold through member brokerage firms just like other securities. The exchanges allow special orders such as price limit orders, market orders, and stop orders for option buyers and sellers. The order process orginates with the broker and is transacted on the floor of an options exchange. For every order there must be both a buyer and a seller or a buyer and a writer so that the orders can be "matched." Once the orders are matched, they are filed with the Options Clearing Corporation. The Options Clearing Corporation then issues the necessary options to the investors. There are four basic transactions handled by the Options Clearing Corporation.

1. Opening Purchase Transaction—a transaction in which an investor intends to become the holder of an option.
2. Opening Sale Transaction—a transaction in which an investor intends to become the seller or writer of an option.
3. Closing Purchase Transaction—a transaction in which an investor who is obligated as a writer of an option intends to terminate his or her obligation as a writer. This accomplished by purchasing and option identical in maturity and strike price to the option that he originally wrote. Such a transaction has the effect, upon acceptance by the Options Clearing Corporation, of canceling the investor's preexisting position as a writer.
4. Closing Sale Transaction—a transaction in which an investor, who is the holder of an outstanding option, intends to liquidate his or her position as a holder. This is accomplished by selling an option of identical strike price and maturity date as the option previously purchased. Such a transaction has the effect upon acceptance by the Options Clearing Corporation of liquidating the investor's preexisting position as holder of the option.

What occurs in any of these transactions is that the holders and writers of options are not contractually linked together, but are committed to the Options Clearing Corporation.

There are no certificates issued for options. A customer must maintain a brokerage account as long as he or she holds an option position and must liquidate the option through the broker originating the transaction in most cases.

If holders of options contracts wish to exercise their option, they must do so through the Options Clearing Corporation. The Options Clearing Corporation will randomly select a writer from all those persons that have written that series of options. This would be true whether the holder chooses to exercise prior to the expiration date or on the expiration date of the option contract. Upon notice of the Options Clearing Corporation, a call writer must sell 100 shares of the underlying common stock at the exercise price, while the put writer must buy 100 shares from the holder exercising the put.

All option contacts are adjusted for stock spilts, stock dividends, or other stock distributions. To summarize where and how to buy options contracts, an investor will initiate all paperwork and transactions with the securities broker. This broker will supply the investor with the Options Clearing Corporation prospectus and will generally be prepared to provide price quotes and other investment advice about the particular option positions of interest to the investor.

HOW TO SELL

As with purchase of options, the investor negotiates the sale of options with the securities broker.

TRANSACTION COSTS

Investors should note that not all securities dealers charge the same fees for services performed. Some firms provide important services for clients over and above the actual execution of a simple buy or sell order. Other firms specialize in offering the lowest possible cost transactions. An individual investor needs to review the level of service he or she requires and select a securities dealer accordingly.

It is not uncommon for small investors to encounter commission charges as high 10 percent or more of the total amount of money invested in option contracts. There is usually a minimum transaction cost of $25 per trade. As an investor increases the quantities of the contracts traded, substantial discounts may be available from all brokerage firms based on the volume of contracts executed in any one order.

PORTFOLIO FIT

The use of options by investors can be very aggressive and risky, or they can be quite conservative and used as a means of reducing risk. Option buyers and writers both attempt to take advantage of the option premium discussed in the preceding section.

Aggressive investors may wish to purchase call options as a means of increasing the leverage in their investment portfolio. Leverage is a very common reason for buying call options when the market is expected to rise during the exercise period of the option contract. The call options are priced much lower than the common stock and the leverage is derived from the small percentage change in the price of the common stock that can cause a very large percentage change in the price of the call option. Table B-3 gives the example of a Federal Express call option.

The options price increase was more than 13 times greater than the stock price increase.

In this same example, as long as the common stock closes under $40, the buyer of the call option loses the entire investment. At a price of $41, the call buyer would break even, as the option is worth an intrinsic value of $1. As the stock price rises past $41, the profit starts accumulating for the call option buyer. If the option contract is sold prior to expiration, the speculative premium may alter the profit potential for the call buyer.

An investor striving for maximum leverage will generally buy options that are "out-of-the-money" or slightly "in-the-money." Buying high-priced options for $10 or $15 that are well "in the

Table B-3
Federal Express $40 October Call Option

Date	Option Price	Stock Price
7/5/84	1.00	34.375
9/5/84	4.25	42.875
Percentage Change in Value	+325%	+24%

money" definitely limits the potential for leverage. An investor may have to commit almost as much in the options contracts as he would to purchase the stocks.

Investors can see from this example that leverage works in both directions. In purchasing call options, if the price of the common stock does not rise, an investor may lose all the invested funds.

A second portfolio use of options contracts is the ownership of call options instead of ownership of common stock. Consider an investor who wishes to own 100 shares of Exxon Corporation with the common stock trading for $50 per share. The investor will receive a tax refund check from the federal government in approximately 90 days for approximately $5,000. However, the investor wants to buy Exxon today in the expectation that during the next 90 days Exxon will appreciate in price. The investor could purchase a call option contract for 100 shares of Exxon and receive any benefits of that price appreciation during that 90-day period until he or she had time to pay for the stock itself. This is referred to as *guaranteeing a price* for purchase of the stock at a later date.

An additional use of options within an investment portfolio is *covered call writing*. The writers of call options take the opposite side of the market from the buyers of call options. The writer is similar to a short seller in that he or she expects the stock to stay at the same price or decline. An option writer who writes covered call options owns the underlying shares of common stock. An option writer that writes "naked" call options does not own the underlying common stock.

Writing covered call options is often considered a hedged position because if the stock price declines, the writer's loss on the stock is partially offset by the option premium. Before writing a covered call option the writer must decide if he or she is willing to sell the underlying stock if it closes above the strike price and the option is exercised.

The use of put options in investment portfolios generally falls into one of three categories. The first category involves the buyer of a put option contract who simply is seeking insurance from price declines in common stocks that he already owns. For example, an investor may have purchased 100 shares of Exxon at $30 several years ago. The market price today has risen to $50. The investor does not wish to sell Exxon shares because the dividend income is desirable. This investor may purchase a put option contract to hedge any price decline in Exxon common stock. The put contract gives the investor the right to sell Exxon holdings for a strike price of $50 per share for a specified period of time in the future.

A second strategy employed by buyers of put option contracts is simply to profit from a bear market or a decline in a particular common stock price. For example, investors may believe that due to price declines in crude oil during the mid-1980s most oil stock prices would decline. An investor seeking to profit from that particular strategy would purchase put contracts without having any ownership position in the common stock. If the price of the stock does decline, the put option contract purchaser should be able to close out this position at a profit.

A third strategy for put option investors is the sale of a put option contract or the writing of a put option contract. This may be done either while the investor owns the underlying common stock or without having the common stock in the portfolio at all. Put writers believe that the price of the common stock will increase over time, thereby causing the put option contract to be worth less money or perhaps to be worth nothing at all upon expiration. For example, the seller of an Exxon 50 put option that expires in April may believe the price of Exxon will rise to $55. If in fact a price rise does occur, the 50 Exxon put would be worthless and the investor would pocket the entire amount of the option premium as a profit from the transaction.

Appendix
C

LIST OF NORTH AMERICAN EXCHANGES

American Stock Exchange
86 Trinity Place
New York, NY 10006
(212) 306-1000

AMEX Commodities Corporation
86 Trinity Place
New York, NY 10006
(212) 306-1000

Chicago Board of Trade
141 W. Jackson Blvd.
Chicago, IL 60604
(312) 435-3500

Chicago Board Options Exchange
La Salle at Van Buren
Chicago, IL 60605
(312) 786-5600

Chicago Mercantile Exchange
30 S. Wacker Drive
Chicago, IL 60606
(312) 930-1000

Chicago Rice & Cotton Exchange
444 W. Jackson Blvd.
Chicago, IL 60606
(312) 341-3078

Coffee, Sugar & Cocoa Exchange, Inc.
4 World Trade Center
New York, NY 10048
(212) 938-2800

Commodity Exchange Inc. (COMEX)
4 World Trade Center
New York, NY 10048
(212) 938-2900

International Monetary Market
Chicago Mercantile Exchange
30 S. Wacker Drive
Chicago, IL 60606
(312) 930-1000

Index and Options Market
Chicago Mercantile Exchange
30 S. Wacker Drive
Chicago, IL 60606
(312) 930-1000

Kansas City Board of Trade
4800 Main Street
Suite 303
Kansas City, MO 64112
(816) 753-7500

Mid America Commodity Exchange
444 W. Jackson Blvd.
Chicago, IL 60606
(312) 341-3000

Minneapolis Grain Exchange
400 S. Fourth Street
Minneapolis, MN 55415
(612) 338-6212

The Montreal Exchange
800 Victoria Square
Montreal H4Z 1A9
(514) 871-2424

New York Cotton Exchange
4 World Trade Center
New York, NY 10048
(212) 938-2702

New York Futures Exchange
20 Broad Street
New York, NY 10005
(212) 623-4949

New York Mercantile Exchange
4 World Trade Center
New York, NY 10048
(212) 938-2222

New York Stock Exchange
11 Wall Street
New York, NY 10005
(212) 623-8533

Pacific Stock Exchange
301 Pine Street
San Francisco, CA 94104
(415) 393-4000

Philadelphia Board of Trade
1900 Market Street
Philadelphia, PA 19103
(215) 496-5025

Philadelphia Stock Exchange
1900 Market Street
Philadelphia, PA 19103
(215) 496-5000

The Toronto Futures Exchange
2 First Canadian Place
The Exchange Tower
Toronto, Ont., Canada MX5 1J2
(416) 947-4700

Toronto Stock Exchange
2 First Canadian Place
The Exchange Tower
Toronto, Ont., Canada MX5 1J2
(416) 947-4700

Vancouver Stock Exchange
609 Granville
Vancouver, B.C., Canada V7Y 1H1
(604) 689-3334

The Winnepeg Commodity Exchange
500 Commodity Exchange Tower
360 Main Street
Winnepeg, Manitoba, Canada R3C 3Z4
(204) 949-0495

Appendix D

BOOKS, PERIODICALS, DATABASES AND OTHER RESOURCES

BOOKS AND PERIODICALS

S&P 100 Index Options: The Index Edge (20 pages)
The Chicago Board Options Exchange
Chicago, IL 60605

Option Pricing and Investment Strategies, Revised Edition
Richard M. Bookstaber
Probus Publishing
Chicago, Illinois 60606

The Options Manual, Third Edition
Gary Gastineau
McGraw-Hill Book Company
New York, NY 10020

How To Make the Market Work for You without Buying a Single Stock: A Basic Guide to SPX (16 pages)
The Chicago Board Options Exchange
Chicago, IL 60605

Stock Index Options, Revised Edition
Donald T. Mesler
Probus Publishing
Chicago, IL 60606

**The Dow Jones-Irwin Guide to Stock Index Futures
and Options**
William Nix & Susan Nix
Dow Jones-Irwin
Homewood, IL 60430

Options as a Strategic Investment, Second Edition
Lawrence G. McMillan
New York Institute of Finance
New York, NY 10270

DATABASES, SOFTWARE AND ON-LINE INFORMATION SERVICES

Note: The vendors listed below offer a combination of services,
including real-time quotations, software and access to historical
records via a database. No endorsement or recommendations are
implied or intended. Contract each vendor for specifics and prices
for the services/products you require.

PC Quote, Inc.
401 South LaSalle Street
Chicago, IL 60605
1-800-225-5657

PC Quote is a comprehensive quote system for stocks, options
and futures delivered in real-time and updated continuously.
PC Quote monitors every major stock, options and futures
exchange—20 exchanges in all.

The options portion of the system includes a constant update
on last sale, net change, bid/ask, contract volume, ticker
symbols and month codes for both puts and calls.

The system offers the user a number of software options that allow users to retrieve, analyze and manipulate data for individual investment purposes.

Users can have access to major databases such as the Dow Jones Newswire or the Associated Press. A technical indicators package is also available. A spreadsheet download function is available, as well as Simultask TM, which allows your personal computer to stay on-line while freeing your computer for spreadsheets, work processing or other tasks.

Hardware supported is limited to some IBM and Compaq models.

Autoquote/PC
CMQ Communications, Inc.
One Financial Plaza
440 South LaSalle Street
Suite 2321
Chicago, IL 60605
1-312-939-7199
FAX 1-312-939-7096

AutoQuote/PC provides access, via a personal computer, to live quotations on 55,000 trading instruments. Information is provided on stocks, bonds, options and futures, and is updated automatically.

AutoQuote/PC is a hardware/software product which runs on the IBM Personal Computer Family, AT&T 6300 or equivalent. A leased line is required for access to information.

AutoQuote/PC does not tie up a personal computer, except for power. A "save" processor handles all communications and maintains a local database.

Users can customize their system to meet specific needs. A variety of news and databases from third party vendors is available.

OPTDAT
National Computer Network
175 W. Jackson
A1038
Chicago, IL 60604
1-312-427-5125

National Computer Network (NCN) is a complete, full-service information center/news retrieval communications network. Among the services offered is a complete database of either real-time or end-of-day information about the major financial markets.

One of the services offered by NCN is OPTDAT, which provides access to all U.S. and Canadian exchanges trading equity and index options contracts. Users have access to historical data as well as all underlying stocks and indexes.

NCN offers a variety of off-the-shelf software packages to facilitate trading. All basic options strategies are available via the SMART software system. The company will also create customized software, tailored to individual needs and specifications.

Options
Warner Computer Systems, Inc.
One University Plaza
Hackensak, NJ 07601
1-102-489-1580

Warner Computer Systems, through its Financial Services Division, provides databases and information services to both institutional and individual customers. The database provides historical records for most major securities, including options. On-line quotations systems are also available for NYSE, AMEX and OTC.

The Options database contains data on all options traded, including such items as price (high, low, close), tickers exchange and more. The data are kept for the life of the option plus one month after the expiration of the option.

Additional hardware and software services are available.

Appendix
E

SOLUTIONS TO END-OF-CHAPTER QUESTIONS

CHAPTER 1

1. An average is the mean value of a group of stocks. The Dow Jones Industrial Average is the most quoted average in the market. An index is a special form of an average. A simple index is an average expressed in terms of a base value.

2. Index weighting is useful to accurately measure the change in an index value caused by a particular stock. In market value weighting, a stock's influence on the index is directly proportional to changes in the stock's market value. Thus, the stock's relative importance in the index is determined by its market value.

   Larger, more important stocks have a greater influence on an index in a weighting scheme. Also, continuous reestimation of the divisor is unnecessary since stock splits, dividends, and conversions are all captured in the market value weighting technique.

3. The major optionable indexes and their objectives are found in Appendix B.

CHAPTER 2

1. The speculator should always follow the speculation guidelines. First, establish the amount *available* for speculation. Second, establish a *realistic* profit objective *before* entering a position. Third, maintain *excess margin* to build flexibility into your positions. Fourth, establish a *market opinion*. If you don't have a strong opinion, don't invest. Fifth, *practice* your strategy thoroughly before actually investing.

2. The primary risk in buying index options is that the option premium will decline. The premium declines with (a) the passage of time, (b) an adverse index movement, and (c) a reduction in index volatility.

   The passage of time hurts option buyers and helps option writers if all other factors are constant.

3. A straddle is the purchase or sale of two options, one put and one call, with the same strike price and the same maturity. A strangle is identical except that two out-of-the-money positions are established. This reduces the risk of the position, but also reduces profitability.

CHAPTER 3

1. A hedging program is meant to reduce the risk associated with an existing position. A stock portfolio may be hedged using index options to protect the value of the portfolio if a market or segment decline is anticipated.

2. A single stock is, on average, riskier than a well-diversified portfolio of stocks. A single stock is affected by both broad market factors such as interest rate changes *and* company-specific factors such as labor strikes. The return on a portfolio of stocks is affected by both of these factors, but the company-specific factors affecting individual stocks tend to cancel each other out.

This risk differential has a great impact on a hedging program. Since the primary risk of a portfolio is related to broad market factors, stock indexes may be used as effective hedging tools.

3. Beta is a measure of the volatility of a single stock relative to the market average. It is important in determining how a stock can be expected to react to a market change. Stocks with high beta react more to a given market movement than do low beta stocks, on average.

4. Correlation is the degree to which two variables coincide. The correlation coefficient measures the magnitude of association. For a hedging program to be successful, you must find an index that is highly correlated with your portfolio. A high correlation is required to ensure that an anticipated market movement has the desired hedging impact.

CHAPTER 4

1. The Options Clearing Corporation is vital to the smooth functioning of the options market. Since all contracts are technically entered into with the OCC, the financial integrity of individual option contractors is unimportant. Without this organization, each option contractor would have to determine the financial capability of his counterpart in the transaction. The efficiency of the market would be hindered dramatically as a result.

2. There are four basic types of options orders. A market order requires the broker to execute transactions at prevailing market prices. Limit orders instruct the broker to transact at a specific price or better. A stop order instructs the broker to make a transaction once a specific price has been reached. Finally, a day order is a limit order good for one trading day only.

4. Settlement risk is incurred because index options are settled one business day after exercise. If the index declines before the option

writer is notified of exercise, the writer is still liable for the value of the index on the exercise date.

5. Other nonprice risks option traders need to consider include trading halts, market liquidity, index adjustments, option opening procedures, and broker insolvency.

Appendix
F

SIMULATION SOLUTIONS

SPECULATION

1. If you expect a rapid change in the market but are uncertain of the direction, either a buy straddle or a buy strangle is appropriate, depending upon your risk preference.

2. If you selected a straddle with a 420 strike and one month to maturity, the call would cost $587.50, the put $287.50, for a total cost of $875 plus $65 commission, or $940. This is the maximum loss position. The maximum gain is theoretically unlimited if the index moves dramatically.

3. The exit decision is a pretransaction profit goal or loss constraint that determines the timing of the closeout. Commonly a position is closed out when a 10 percent loss or a 30 percent gain has been sustained.

4. The value of the straddle is now $1268.75. Since this represents nearly a 35 percent gain, the exit decision has been activated.

5. To close out the position, notify your broker using one of the orders described in Chapter 4 (market, limit, etc.). Your broker will notify you when the deal has been completed on the option exchange.

6. The profit on the position is now $172.50 (the total value of the straddle is now $1112.50) for a return of about 18 percent.

HEDGING SIMULATION

1. The beta of this portfolio is approximately 1.05 on a market value weighted basis. The beta describes the average volatility of the portfolio relative to the market. This portfolio is, on average, about 5 percent more volatile than the market.

2. Since the primary goal is protection of the portfolio without sacrificing upside potential, the appropriate hedging tool is a protective put.

3. The correlation coefficients between the portfolio and the S & P 100, S & P 500, and the Major Market Index are .886, .842, and .764, respectively. The statistics indicate that there is roughly a 90 percent correlation between the portfolio and the S & P 100. This is the index that should be used for hedging the portfolio at this point in time.

4. To determine the number of options purchased, divide your portfolio value ($245,340) by the contract value of the put options (238.78 × $100 = $23,878) and multiply by the portfolio beta (1.05). The total number of options required using this formula is 10.78, or 11.

5. Purchasing the first out-of-the-money put provides good protection against a sharp decline in the market at a relatively low cost. Thus, 11 Jan 235 strike puts are purchased for a total of $4537.50 plus $65 commission for a total cost of $4602.50. If a higher strike

option were selected, more protection would be purchased, but at a significantly higher cost. Conversely, a lower strike option would provide limited coverage at a minimal cost.

6. First, a system for obtaining information on the hedge should be established before entering the transaction. Second, the market opinion of the hedger should be rechecked. For this hedge to be effective, a significant market decline must be expected. Finally, the hedge exit decision should be set.

7. The hedge should be removed if your market opinion becomes more favorable. Even if the market declines, the hedge may be altered if the portfolio and hedging index move in opposite directions. This unusual situation could be very profitable (if the index fell and the portfolio rose) or very risky (if the index rose and the portfolio fell).

8. The current price of each put is $325 which, multiplied by 11 is $3575. The options position closed with a loss of $1027.50. Since the portfolio value at this time equaled $246,000 (a gain of $660), the net loss on the portfolio was $367.50. If the portfolio was unhedged, the full $246,000 could have been lost. In this situation a significant market decline did not occur. If it had, the hedge would have been more effective. Thus, the slow market decline is the worst possible scenario for this hedge.

9. The profits/losses on the options are considered current gains or losses. Profits/losses on the portfolio (if unchanged) are classified as capital gains or losses.

Appendix
G

ABOUT THE AUTHOR

MIKEL T. DODD is a principal in a Washington, D.C. based investment company. In addition, he is an extensive speaker and writer on the subject of investments. Dodd has a Ph.D. in finance from the University of Arkansas and was formerly an Assistant Professor of Finance at the School of Business Administration, Georgetown University, Washington, D.C.

About the Publisher

PROBUS PUBLISHING COMPANY

Probus Publishing Company fills the informational needs of today's business professional by publishing authoritative, quality books on timely and relevant topics, including:

- Investing
- Futures/Options Trading
- Banking
- Finance
- Marketing and Sales
- Manufacturing and Project Management
- Personal Finance, Real Estate, Insurance and Estate Planning
- Entrepreneurship
- Management

Probus books are available at quantity discounts when purchased for business, educational or sales promotional use. For more information, please call the Director, Corporate/Institutional Sales at 1-800-PROBUS-1, or write:

Director, Corporate/Institutional Sales
Probus Publishing Company
1925 N. Clybourn Avenue
Chicago, Illinois 60614
FAX (312) 868-6250